Ain't No Such Animal

...and other stories from
the Ozarks hills

Larry Dablemont
Illustrations by Tom Goldsmith

BARNABAS
PUBLISHING SERVICES

Ain't No Such Animal...and other stories from the Ozark hills

Illustrations by
Tom Goldsmith

Editing and designing
Hope V. Stewart

ISBN: 1-892477-09-2
Library of Congress Cataloging in Publication Number: 98-74747

Table of Contents

Acknowledgements

I want to thank Reta and Hope Stewart for doing the publishing work on this book, Canadian artist Tom Goldsmith for doing the illustrations and Gloria Jean, the world's second- or third-greatest secretary-wife for taking handwritten stories and making them into readable manuscripts. And most of all, I'd like to thank all those Ozark people who read my outdoor columns in various newspapers and take the time to let me and the newspapers know they are reading them.

A word from the author

Someone once asked me when it was that I first wanted to become a writer. Well, I never did want to be a writer, I always wanted to be a game warden, or a forest ranger when I was young. But I have been writing stories about the outdoors since I was in the third grade. A third grade teacher in the Houston, Missouri grade school, Violet Frost, noticed that I was always writing poems and stories in my Big Chief tablet, so she assembled some of them and had them printed up in a little book with a blue cover, and had me going around from room to room reading them to older kids in the 4th and 5th grade. Some of those older kids still hated me in high school for putting them through that.

Any encouragement I received as a writer ended there. I went to college my first two years at School of the Ozarks and took one writing course which I nearly failed. Then I transferred to University of Missouri and studied wildlife management, hoping to become a biologist. While there, an advisor in the wildlife department helped me get into some writing classes in the prestigious Missouri School of Journalism where people like Tennessee Williams had studied. I was barely passing when I dropped the class. I would write something, get a poor grade on it, and then sell it to some small outdoor magazine just as I had written it. Finally, the instructor and I had a meeting, and he told me that since I was from the School of Agriculture, I was not about to get grades competitive with his Journalism students. Then he gave me the best advice I've ever received. "Why are you trying to learn how to write in my class," he said. "If you are selling your material, keep doing what you are doing!"

That year in college I wrote an article about an old wooden john-boat I had used as a boy on the Big Piney river back home. What happened with that story was sort of miraculous. I sent it to Outdoor Life magazine and they bought it. I think back then it brought about a thousand dollars. Keep in mind that while at University of Missouri, I paid my way through school working 30 hours a week at two jobs for about $1.25 per hour. Then a New York Publishing company, which produced an annual book entitled, The Best Sports Stories of the Year, picked "Old Paint" as the best outdoor story of 1973, and published it in their book. One of the judges actually said it was "the best magazine writing of the lot." So then I decided I WAS a writer! — I've learned better since. I know nothing about writing — can't tell anyone how to do it, and don't know a participle from a predicate. If you've read my stuff in the past, you know that already. But "Old Paint" is the second story in this book, the story which got me started with Outdoor Life magazine — the first major manuscript I ever sold. When I read it just before putting this book together, I was tempted to rewrite it... but I didn't. In fact, I have pretty much left these stories as they were originally published. Because of that some of them may sound a little puzzling... they are dated. And you may occasionally see similar themes and descriptions of events in two different articles.

"Ain't No Such Animal" is my dad's story of an event during his boyhood, which I wrote for him and it was published in Outdoor Life in the mid 1970's. Others which appeared in Outdoor Life are, "The Big Deer Bet" 1994... "The Ghost Gobbler"...late 1980s.... "Old Fighter," about 1974. Petersen's Hunting magazine published some of these stories, "Come November," 'First Gobbler," "Silent Jack and the Master," "He Loves to Watch 'em Fly" and "The Shoot-off" all in the 1980s. When that magazine published it's "Best of Fifty Years" publication, the latter story was chosen for inclusion.

Most of the other stories were published by other magazines at one time or another. "Fargo" is one of the most recent, published in "The Pointing Dog Journal" in 1996. "The Relentless Pursuit" is one of the oldest, published in a long forgotten magazine known as "The Missouri Sportsman" about 1973. You'll love the old black and white picture of my grandpa and the giant catfish in "Catfish That Size Never Die." Grandpa caught that fish the night I was born, and never caught a larger one ever.

Several of these stories are first person fiction. They are based on real people and actual events, but are fictitious stories. They are; "The Big Deer Bet," "Tommy's Brother," "Fargo," "first Gobbler" and "He Jus' Loves To Watch 'Em Fly."

Two of these stories are newly written, and have never been seen before. "The Blizzard on Netley Marsh" is the only story which takes place out of the Ozarks, and probably should have been placed in another book sometime. But it is a good adventure story. The other one is the Christmas story, "Miracle on a Snowy River," which has a message in it you may have to think about for awhile. Both these stories were written last year, 1997. The latter one was written after a Springfield, Missouri newspaper editor told me I could not mention God in my weekly outdoor column. I sat down, angry because God couldn't be included in my newspaper material, and wrote the piece for a magazine. Then I realized I had written something which there was no market for. I think it will fit here just fine.

So what this book ends up being is a celebration of 25 years of magazine writing: 1972 to 1997. And if anyone asks you, it is a book compiled by an outdoorsman who writes, not a writer. Hopefully there will be more to come... maybe a book including 25 years of selected newspaper outdoor columns. And I still think "Poems for the Duck Hunter" would make a great book!

Dad had been setting steel traps along the Big Piney since he was 15. He had made a name for himself with the F. C. Taylor Fur Company in St. Louis. In the late 1920s he had in three successive years brought in record catches for an individual trapper. That last year he was the subject of a full-page feature in the St. Louis Globe newspaper.

Finally, hospitalized from overexertion and exposure, he was forced to restrain his outdoor life. But he never turned away from the outdoors as a means of support. We lived with the land.

To many people, it was a disgraceful way to live. In those days, hunting and fishing were not the acclaimed and glamorous pastimes they are today. In the Ozarks, "sportsman" was a little-used term.

At 14, I was beginning to want things that the town kids had. I had a bicycle, but the back wheel had no spokes, and when I rode it the wheel looked as if it was about to fold up. I got laughed at on occasion, riding my bicycle along the dirt road that led to the nearest town, Houston, six miles away.

Dad said if I did well with my traps, maybe there'd be a little money left over to buy a new bicycle wheel. That was enough to build my enthusiasm as the trapping season approached.

Dad's trap lines would be on the lower Piney and Gasconade where there were more furbearers. He would move his traps regularly and spend a lot of time camping. When he returned home to replace traps, store stretched pelts, and renew supplies, it was often only for a day or so.

I'd be running my own small line in the eddies near our home. One long eddy known as the Mill Pond Eddy was formed by the small mill dam where we lived. Below it, were a series of rapids and two long eddies known as the Sweet Potato Hole and the Ginseng Eddy. Past the Ginseng was a long, narrow stretch of water flanked by low bluffs and rock outcroppings. A half mile below, the McKinney Eddy sprawled out below a great bluff whose sheer face jutted into the river.

By opening day of trapping season in November, I had traps and stretching boards ready. A few days earlier

Dad had spent a Saturday teaching me the fine points of trapping. I had run lines with him often, but there was a lot more I had to learn.

"A muskrat is easy to catch," Dad told me as we moved up the Mill Pond Eddy that crisp morning, surrounded by the last of the blazing fall colors.

"He's not as smart as a mink, don't mind the scent of man, and don't pay much attention to a trap."

I had 15 small single-spring traps, and Dad showed me how to set them.

Dad always used a drown-set. We set each trap on a log or in a den or in the shallows along the bank and wired the end of the trap chain to a rock, which we placed in water deep enough to drown the fur bearer. When caught, muskrats, coons, and mink, will struggle against the trap only momentarily, then will swim toward midstream and drown under the weight of the trap and chain.

Dad told me that day that while muskrats are easy to catch, it takes an experienced trapper to catch a mink. He said that a mink could be caught by a smart trapper along a bluff that jutted out into the river at the base.

"When he comes to that sheer rock bluff, he'll always go into the water right at the edge of it," Dad said, hauling out a big double-spring trap, stout enough to hold a mink. "And then he'll swim around it and come out at the other side, right at the edge again. So you set traps on both sides."

At the edge of the bluff at the McKinney eddy, Dad showed me the basics of fooling a mink, making it plain that it would be a few years before I'd be able to do it. I watched him don gloves and burn off the trap over a small fire upstream from the bluff. Then he carefully placed the trap beside the bluff under a couple of inches of water. Finally he gathered leaves and grass from the river-bottom and, bit by bit, covered the trap and chain. When he finished, it looked as if they had settled there naturally.

Hiding those traps with leaves was a natural talent of Dad's. In all my years of trapping that followed, I never learned how to copy it, nor did I know anyone who could.

Mom was worried about my new venture. I'd be rising before daylight in order to run trap lines and get to school on time. In the evening I had to do my regular chores, then skin and stretch pelts and run to reset my traps again. It didn't leave much time for homework.

I hurried home from school on opening day and loaded my traps aboard the old john-boat. I had 13 single-spring traps and two double-springs. I paddled to the upper end of the Mill Pond eddy and set a pair of traps, then headed downstream. I set the last two traps at the base of the bluff at the McKinney eddy. They were the double-springs, placed where I knew there was a chance to get a mink.

Paddling back home that evening against the current of the Piney, I felt a part of the river. It didn't seem important just then that my math lessons weren't up to par. Running a trap line wasn't something I'd get graded on, but it was something I meant to learn.

At the last shoal between me and home, I watched a flock of wood ducks wing in and drop from sight over the sycamores at the head of the Mill Pond eddy. They'd be there come dawn. I'd have brought back some for supper if I hadn't been so busy with my traps.

I tied my boat to the big oak below the house and clambered up the bank, shuffling noisily through fallen leaves. The work was over for a time. Now came the waiting.

An Ozarks dawn in November is something a fellow never forgets. The mist rises in columns from the water and shrouds the pines along the bluffs.

That's the way it was the second morning of that season in 1940. My overalls soaked up the dew on the boat seat as I paddled up to the head of the Mill Pond eddy in the early morning grayness. The wood ducks were where I thought they'd be, back in the pocket above the bluff where they could find acorns in the quiet water. They left with the drum of wings, one old hen squawking discontentedly, shattering the stillness of the river.

My first trap was no longer on the end of the log. I'd caught a nice muskrat with my first effort. I fished him from The river and moved downstream to my remaining traps.

Of the 13 single-spring traps, five held muskrats. The double-spring traps at the base of the bluff at the McKinney eddy were undisturbed.

I skinned my pelts that evening and stretched them as I had seen Dad do so often. The sock-like pelts, flesh side out, would dry on the ironing board shaped stretching boards.

Dad returned the next evening and helped me with six more muskrats I had taken. He had several "rats" too, but a pair of big coons and a nice mink caught my attention. I told him of the trap in a den just down from the house that had taken a muskrat both mornings.

"A den like that," Dad said, "you'll probably have another'n before bedtime."

Three hours after dark, I checked that trap and had another muskrat. I reset the trap and returned to the house where Dad was reading by a kerosene lantern.

"I'll set the alarm clock and catch another yet tonight," I told him as I prepared to turn in.

He turned from his reading and looked solemnly toward me. "Don't get greedy son. In sight of two weeks you'll have all the muskrats outa this stretch o' river anyway. What you'll need more'n anything'll be yore sleep."

By the end of the first two weeks I had caught 23 muskrats. My take had dropped off, as Dad had predicted, but finally those two double-spring traps at the McKinney eddy made up for the slack.

It was a cold morning and my breath formed a cloud of vapor as I moved downstream. When I found that both of the big traps were missing, I got really excited. I was thinking of a mink, but couldn't imagine one strong enough to pull away traps, chains, and rocks.

After 20 minutes of searching, I found a big boar coon in the middle of the eddy in water so deep I could barely see him. I'd miss school to get him, but it had to be done, so I paddled back home and got a big trotline hook and a length of trotline. Returning to the McKinney eddy, I hauled up my first raccoon, worth nearly $10.

With time to spare, I began looking for new places to set my traps. Between the Ginseng eddy and the McKinney hole, in the long stretch of narrow water and shoals, I came across a huge mink track on a mud flat just below a small rock ledge that extended into the water. It was a perfect place for the two double-spring traps. I set them there, working tediously with gloved hands to hide the submerged traps with leaves that would appear to have settled there. Clouds were moving in, but I was so intent on catching that mink, I gave them little heed.

Dad did. He was home at dusk.

"Took up my traps today," he said. "Rain's movin' in -- maybe a flood. Hope you got yours in."

I was startled by the realization that I had failed to read the coming rain and what it would mean.

At dusk the rain began to pelt down in big heavy drops. I prepared to go after my trap line, but Dad forbade it.

"We'll get most of 'em after the water comes back down," he said. "The ones you lose will be a lesson to you. From here out, you'll do without 'em."

Ashamed, I turned in early that night I listened to the rain pelt the roof above my attic bed. Drifting into uneasy sleep, I seemed to hear the river roaring with swollen waters already. I had lost my chance at the big mink and my chance to prove I was a trapper.

I awakened to the sound of a slow, steady drizzle. The weather was much colder, and the river had a three-foot rise on it. Icicles were beginning to form on limbs.

Dad was bringing in firewood as I hurried down the ladder. He rubbed his hands together and knelt to rekindle the fire in the old potbellied stove.

"Winter's shore 'nuff hit," he said. "Gonna be ice all over if it keeps up."

We worked around the cabin for a day or so, preparing, stacking, and bundling pelts we'd soon be showing to fur buyers. By the fourth day after the rain, the Piney was clear again but still a little high and icy.

I found nine of my 13 single-spring traps. But in the narrow chute before the Ginseng eddy, both of my double spring traps were gone.

There was a big drift of logs and limbs not far downstream from the overhanging rock. I knew my traps were probably in the drift, so I dug in. Halfway inside, I came across a piece of wire and an empty trap. I worked in farther and spotted part of my second trap underwater beneath the drift. When I pulled it free, it brought with it the carcass of mink.

He was enormous, but caked with mud and debris. I felt like crying. I knew he would be worthless by now, and I'd rather never have known he existed than see him ruined.

Ironically, I almost certainly would never have caught the mink but for the flood. It surely hid my trap enough to fool him as I never could have done with my inexperience.

Returning home, I felt sick inside. The huge mink lay across the boat seat, completely wasted.

When Dad saw the mink, he stared at it for what seemed an eternity. I waited, afraid to speak. I knew Dad hated to waste anything.

Shaking his head, he finally exclaimed, "Lord, what a mink!"

He lifted it up and examined it, his face still registering disbelief. "Biggest ever I seen." He knelt at the edge of the river and washed the mud from the slick fur. "Don't believe the pelt is hurt at all," he said.

My heart jumped.

Finally Dad straightened and held the mink high, fur now glossy, making the animal appear even larger.

"Damn!" Dad said, shaking his head again, "Yore the luckiest kid ever I knowed, any way you look at it. This pelt is still good."

Apparently the cold water had preserved the mink.

I was elated as I helped dad carefully skin and stretch the magnificent pelt. Dad was happy about it, too, and he speculated the fur would be graded No. 1, large, worth about $38.

"Maybe," I ventured, "it's an extra large."

Dad gave me a solemn look and said, "Told you onc't, they ain't no such animal."

By December several fur buyers had been by our home on the river to look at the cache of furs Dad had in

7

the smokehouse.

I had 29 muskrats, a coon and that big mink, which drew the immediate attention and exclamation of each buyer. Dad had more than 70 muskrats, four mink, and about a dozen coons. According to the price list from the F. C. Taylor Fur Company in St. Louis (the company has since moved to Louisville, Kentucky), we should have almost $400 worth of fur. The best offer we received from a fur buyer was $60 short of that.

In previous years my older brother, Norten, had taken our furs to St. Louis by bus to sell directly to the company. But Norten was gone now, and Dad faced a dilemma. He needed the money for Christmas, but he couldn't afford to sell to a local buyer when St. Louis fur houses offered more money. Dad didn't want to leave his trap line for a day, but he hesitated to send me to handle family business in a jungle I had never seen before.

Eventually, he decided he had no choice, and at my urging he agreed to let me go.

Less than two weeks before Christmas, I got up before dawn and rode into nearby Houston with a neighbor. Over 100 pelts had been bound tightly and wrapped in two bundles. They smelled a little, but at 7 a.m. there weren't many people on the bus. The driver helped me pack them away in the back.

It took over four hours to get to St. Louis. The bus stop was bustling with activity when we arrived just before noon. I carried the furs inside and ate a quick sandwich, still awed by the surroundings. A few minutes later I strained to shove the furs into a taxi and gave the driver a slip of paper with the address of the F. C. Taylor Fur Company on it.

I was at the fur company's big brick building before the noon lunch break had ended. I was told to relax and wait. The whole place smelled of furs -- familiar and not unpleasant odors to me. Despite the roar of traffic outside, I felt better. I had gotten there safely.

Eventually, I wound up on the second floor, with The bundles of fur on a big table before me. It seemed colder in the building than it did outside.

I moved around looking at other piles of fur until a

man arrived with some price lists and a notebook. He was a large, heavy fellow with a big black mustache. At the time I imagined that he was Mr. Taylor himself. He asked me my name as he began to go through Dad's furs. When I told him, he smiled.

"I knew it," he said. "I always recognize that man's furs." Then he looked up at me. "Nobody prepares a pelt like your dad, son. He's the best there is."

He examined each pelt quickly and called out sizes and prices to an assistant who wrote them dawn on a sheet of paper. Thirty minutes later he had finished with Dad's furs and began looking at mine. I held my breath as he moved toward the last pelt, that of my mink. When he uncovered it he simply stopped, and for a moment his face was expressionless. Then he issued a low whistle. "Is that a mink!" he exclaimed, shaking his head.

He called another man over and together they admired the pelt, turning it inside and out repeatedly. Finally he looked at me. "You say this is your pelt? You caught this mink?"

I nodded, trying to look nonchalant.

"Well, Son" he said. You've brought in the biggest mink I've ever seen." He turned to his assistant and said, "Mink, number one, extra large..."

As the bus rolled back to Houston, I slept. The anxiety was over, the furs were no longer mine to worry about, and secure in the folds of my hand-me-down billfold was a check for $423. Dad had instructed me not to sell for less than $375. I was proud to be coming home with a sizable amount over that. But I was just as proud of the list in my pocket with the price and grade of each pelt the company had bought. At the bottom of the list was my mink, the biggest one they'd ever seen at St. Louis.

The bus got back to Houston after 8 p.m., and I walked part way home before a neighbor gave me a ride.

Two days later Dad brought his trap line home, just in front of flying clouds and a chill in the air that told him a bad spell was coming.

Dad wasn't one to let his feelings show much, but he couldn't hide his pleasure. This Christmas there would be

9

things the family needed -- shoes, clothes and maybe even a toy gun for each of my younger brothers. I was thinking of a new bicycle wheel, but I hated to ask.

Several days after my return from the city I was helping dad prepare pelts.

"You did quite a job for your first try at trappin'," he said, not looking up from his work. "Guess you earned that new bicycle wheel. With that line of yours you made ninety-eight dollars."

Puzzled, I looked up.

"No," I objected, "I made a hundred and forty two. You aren't counting the mink."

"What mink?" Dad asked, his voice all but expressionless.

"The one I caught," I said. "The number one extra large."

Dad looked up from the stretching board and reached deep into his overalls pockets. When he withdrew his hand it was clutching a wad of bills. A grin played at the corners of his mouth as he handed me the $44 my mink had brought.

"I told you twice already," he said, "they ain't no such animal."

It's said the day of the trapper is gone forever, and I reckon it is. I can't say I'm sorry. In later years I gave up trapping for good, and so did Dad. The prices for furs plummeted after 1945 (though recently they've come back strong for some furs), but that's not the real reason Dad quit. As he grew older he just got to where he could no longer live with the thought of putting a furbearer through the torture of a steel trap.

A drown-set kills quickly, and that's all we ever used. I realize, as I'm sure Dad did, that death by drowning is no more cruel or slow than the natural death a mink or muskrat might meet at the hands of a predator, disease, or starvation. And for this reason I can't go along with those who wish to ban the use of steel traps.

Many opponents of steel traps are landowners who profess concern for fur bearers. Yet a lot of these landowners methodically cut down trees along the river and destroy natural habitat. Which is worse?

Today, there are not as many muskrats along the Big Piney as there were in 1940. One reason for it is the great increase in numbers of their main predator, the mink. It's not unusual at all to see a family of mink along the river today. And the beaver, with trapping pressure gone, has exploded all across the Ozarks. Most streams are overpopulated with them. Perhaps a few old-time trappers could be of benefit in helping to harvest some of the excess numbers.

I'll never trap again, but if there is another youngster along the Piney who wants to set a line along the river this winter, I'm for him.

My dad and two younger brothers with furs taken in 1936 at our fishing camp on the Big Piney River.

more rapids roaring just around the bend. Old Paint responded easily to each silent stroke of Dad's paddle.

We hadn't gone far when Dad spotted a lone mallard feeding among some fallen leaves in the quiet shallows along the bank. I watched through the blind as we floated closer to the unsuspecting mallard.

With a powerful stroke of the paddle, Dad quickly turned the boat sideways. He dropped his paddle and then reached for his gun as the startled mallard took off. The gun roared, and the greenhead folded and dropped. At that moment, a big fox squirrel darted from the water's edge and scampered to the high branches of a big maple.

Dad usually passed up squirrels if he thought that the shot would alarm ducks farther downriver. But this time my father had already fired once, so he shot the squirrel. The dead bushytail fell to a fork in the tree, about 20 feet above the ground.

My family has always relished wild meat, and Dad was never one to waste game. He climbed the tree to retrieve the squirrel while I watched from below.

Dad is a big man, standing six feet two inches; in those days he weighed 200 pounds. The branch he was standing on moved a little when he reached for the squirrel, and Dad lost his footing. He grabbed for a limb and then crashed to the ground while I watched in stunned silence.

Dad landed hard on some big tree roots that stuck out from the bank. He rolled into the water, and at first I thought he was dead. With a strength beyond that of an 11-year-old, I pulled my father from the water and then helped him to crawl up the bank to level ground. He rolled on his back and gasped with pain. His face was covered with blood from a cut over his eye, and he was spitting even more blood. Years have not dulled my memory of that moment.

Dad must have known that I was ready to panic, but he managed to calm me down and sent me to a nearby road for help. I found the road, and a passing motorist stopped, took charge, and rushed Dad to a doctor.

That afternoon, a friend of the family took me back to the river to get our boat and equipment. He let me out on the highway so I could fetch the boat and float it downstream to a farm road where the craft would be taken out. I didn't stay long at the scene of Dad's accident, but I can still remember the dried blood on the leaves where he had lain. Otherwise, the river was calm and peaceful, and the day had warmed considerably.

I paddled Old Paint for the first time then, with Dad's shotgun beside me. I remember thinking that the first trip in the new boat might have been the last for Dad. As it turned out, Dad didn't use the new boat again until the next spring. He was laid up several weeks with three broken ribs and a punctured lung plus some minor injuries. But some good times were to come with Old Paint.

To a family that lived with the river as mine did, john-boats were tools of the trade. Dad's father, Fred Dablemont, had raised four sons on the Big Piney, six miles from Houston and deep in the south-central, Missouri Ozarks. The Dablemonts lived the lives of rivermen, trapping in the winter, selling fish and bullfrogs in the summer, and guiding parties of hunters and fishermen year-round. Grandpa was active on the Big Piney until a few months before his death in 1970, at the age of 74.

Rivermen depended on sturdy, stable, and easy-to-handle boats, and Grandpa made the best. Like boat builders in other parts of the Ozarks, Grandpa had his own special pattern for his products; he called them "sharpshooters." The name john-boat apparently was coined by someone other than the men who first built such boats. The craft might just about as easily have been known as pirogues, or even as wooden canoes. The large 20-foot john-boats were developed for big Ozarks rivers like the Current, White and Gasconade. But on smaller streams such as the Piney, shorter boats were better. Grandpa's sharpshooters were usually 14 feet long, not built for motors, but designed to be handled with a stout sassafras paddle. My family grew up with the home-built boats and could do things with a boat paddle that I've never seen equaled.

Besides the boats that they made for their own use, Grandpa and his sons sold their john-boats, as many as 25 of them in a summer, to aspiring floaters in three states. The going rate for Grandpa's john-boats was $25 apiece in the

1920s and '30s. Dad sold his first john-boats in the 1950s for $35 each. In the 1960s, the price went up to $50 because of increasing lumber costs.

Transportation was limited in the early days, and the Dablemonts didn't haul their boats back upstream by road after a float trip. If Grandpa or his sons took a party on a float trip one day, they ran the boat back upriver the next day. They could go upstream over a riffle just deep enough for the boat.

There was no such thing as switching sides with a boat paddle. The Dablemonts would paddle from one side, maneuvering the boat for miles without a sound and without lifting the paddle from the water.

The wooden boats could be operated so quietly that it was easy to stack some tree limbs on the bow, arrange some branches to hide the boat's occupants, and sneak up on a flock of ducks, a watering deer, or any other wildlife.

The john-boats were tough and maneuverable, as well as quiet. The craft could take hard knocks and could slide easily over rocks. The high-floating boats were practically impossible to swamp, and they responded to the lightest touch of the paddle.

The metal boats and canoes of recent years are lighter than old-fashioned john-boats, and the modern craft are fine for joyriding. But when it comes to landing a 40-pound flathead catfish on trotline in the middle of the night, or running a trapline on a rough river in zero-degree weather, a man doesn't want a canoe; and when a successful duck-hunting or floatfishing trip depends on silence and the best possible concealment, a man doesn't want aluminum, or so Grandpa always said. Grandpa and Dad made their boats sleek, strong and dependable. Old Paint was no exception.

The spring after Dad's accident, we took the boat to the Ginseng eddy, one of the most beautiful spots on the Piney. Three big, deep eddies were filled with several species of fish. I was there practically every day, usually late in the evening when the high ridge shadowed the river and everything was quiet and peaceful. Alone, I would maneuver Old Paint through those eddies, fishing my favorite spots for bass, bluegill and goggle-eye (rockbass).

I learned to handle a boat well that summer, though I still lacked the strength to do many things that would come later. I also learned that the river was important not only to me, but also to the other forms of life that seemed so busy while I relaxed in the middle of the stream, waiting for a strike. A family of young mink regularly showed up at the base of the big bluff, playfully chasing one another or eyeing the brood of wood ducks that hurriedly followed their anxious mother to the cover of the opposite bank. A kingfisher was always nearby, sounding upset about something, but always ready to plunge to the river in search of an easy meal. And on rare occasions, I could see a big old smallmouth bass that lurked in the depths and was just too smart to be caught. That was a summer for learning, and appreciating.

By the next fall, in 1959, I had a gun of my own to carry — a single-shot Iver Johnson. The ducks and squirrels were thick on the river that year. Dad and I hunted quite often then with Dad's cousin, Charley. We had some memorable hunts, but the one that we'll remember occurred in December on the last weekend of the season. The river was high and treacherous, and the temperature was blue-cold — somewhere in the low 20s. Ice was everywhere — hanging from limbs that dipped into the water, lying in sheets along the surface of the quiet backwater areas, and even encrusted on the blades of the boat paddles.

At 10 a.m. we headed into a long stretch of water with Cousin Charley handling the boat. Around a bend, a fallen tree jutted across the river, and the current slammed into the log head-on with a roar. Water splashed up and over the downed trunk. Charley could have avoided the log easily enough by cutting out of the current and into the dead water, but when he applied power to the paddle, the blade caught between two large rocks and then snapped off.

We hit the tree seconds later. Old Paint leaned, and water poured in over the side. I went overboard and under the water for a moment, still clutching my precious shotgun. But Dad, who had leaped from the boat with his own gun a second earlier, grabbed me and hauled me to the bank.

17

Shocked and numbed by the cold, I watched Dad return to the chest-deep current to help Charley pull Old Paint away from the log. If the boat had sunk in the fast water close to the log, the two men couldn't have dragged the craft free of the tremendous current.

None of our equipment had been dumped. Old Paint had remained precariously upright, though the boat was nearly filled with water. We had lost only one thing: Charley's new Winchester automatic shotgun!

Dad ordered me to run up and down the bank to keep my blood circulating. Every movement was torture; my clothes had instantly turned stiff with ice, and the cold both numbed and burned me at the same time.

Fortunately we had a lighter but the wood was damp. Dad and Charley poured the powder from several shells onto the gravel bar and then dug dead leaves and twigs from drift-piles. The powder was touched off, and the flash ignited the leaves at once; small twigs dried and slowly began to burn. We gradually built the small blaze into a bonfire and then we stripped down to insulated underwear.

Charley returned to the icy current and began searching for his gun. On the third dive, he came up with his gun and a grin that defied the cold water.

Our clothes dried slowly as we stood, half-naked before the blaze, roasting on one side and freezing on the other. Eventually, we got underway again.

A few months later, and suddenly it was spring again. Old Paint and I went into the floatfishing business. We had a grand old time, taking people on float trips and making 75 cents an hour for the services of the two of us. As a river guide, I began to gain valuable experience. I didn't have a great many clients, but business picked up as word got around.

Some of my clients got wet. One fellow jumped from the boat when a water snake dropped from an overhanging limb; another man was swept overboard by a low branch that he had failed to duck. I didn't have the strength yet to be a top-notch guide, but Old Paint helped me by staying upright.

Several years rolled past, and Old Paint and I kept

on floating. I didn't go to Houston High School parties or to other social affairs, because I preferred the river, running trotlines in the company of Old Paint and a cousin who became my fishing partner.

Old Paint and I were working the entire river from mouth to source by then. In 1962, when I turned 15, one of my floatfishing clients, a lady fisherman who was as green at the sport as a spring sapling, hooked into the big smallmouth that I had been still trying to catch in the Ginseng eddy. Old Fighter, as we called the fish, must have had some anxious moments at the end of the lady's line. But in the end, the bass took my clients's plug back with him to the depths of the Ginseng Eddy. The lady didn't cry, as I expected her to do. Instead, she was ecstatic merely because she had seen the fish and had fought him awhile. I learned something about sportsmanship that day.

I had another client that summer whom I remember well. He came down from the University of Missouri, and though I don't recall his name, I'll always remember his advice. When I told the man about the river — the fish, the bullfrogs, and great blue heron — he told me that I should become something called a naturalist. Though I didn't know what a naturalist was, I soon found out, and the desire to become a naturalist was the force that helped a poor country boy to get a college degree. I later became Chief Naturalist for Arkansas State Parks, and an outdoor columnist for the *Arkansas Gazette.*

By my last year in high school, Old Paint was getting along in years, for a john-boat. The wooden boat was getting water-soaked and heavy, and though we had newer john-boats by then, Old Paint remained my favorite.

That spring, I moved Old Paint to a big eddy on the upper end of the Piney at the mouth of Hog Creek, where I did a lot of trotlining for big flatheads.

I dedicated my efforts to the rugged sport for one month that summer, and I was rewarded with catfish weighing 10, 15, 18, 24 and 26 pounds. All of the big cats came from below the big white bluff that towers over the eddy.

I let my floatfishing business taper off that summer, and I tried some plug fishing. I caught some big bass at Hog

Creek, one largemouth weighed nearly eight pounds. But I left Old Paint at Hog Creek a little too long. Inconsiderate floaters shot holes in the aging boat. I brought Old Paint home for repair, patching the holes and a crack in one side, and then added a fourth coat of drab green paint. Dad, who saw little reason to put more effort into the old boat since we had better ones, gave it the name that still sticks in my mind.

"Not much left of this boat but patches and old paint." Dad sighed, examining the boat and shaking his head.

Soon afterward, I enrolled at the School of the Ozarks, and I was away from the Big Piney the first time in my life. In 1967, I began studying wildlife management at the University of Missouri. My quest for a formal education claimed me for five days a week, but come Friday evening I'd hitchhike home to refresh and relax my mind on the river —fishing, hunting, or just floating in the old john-boat. Old Paint was beginning to leak a little, but it still floated high and responded well to each stroke of the paddle. In 1969, my third year of college, disaster struck. I arrived early one Friday afternoon for a nearly-spring camping trip, but Dad had rented Old Paint to a St. Louis man who was floating the river with two sons. The floaters were expected to return before dark, but as so often happens in the Ozarks, storm clouds turned the sunny day to gray, and darkness came early. The torrent of rain that followed raised the river slowly for two hours before the storm ended as quickly as it had begun.

Dad and I were worried about the floaters, and we went to the take-out point. I hiked upriver in search of the party. I had often sat out storms in caves along the river, but these floaters were inexperienced and unfamiliar with the Big Piney.

The man and his sons could have passed the take-out point, for the river had become higher and much faster. Or the party could have swamped the boat in the swift current. I returned by dark, sure that the people were in trouble. By then the Piney was rolling nearly five feet above normal and was still rising.

Dad hurried back to check at the hotel, but there had been no word from the floaters. We notified the authorities and began organizing a search party. But the St. Louis man finally called from a farmhouse four miles below the scheduled take-out point that he and his sons had missed in the storm.

The search was called off, and we hurried to the river to bring back the wet and weary floaters. In his haste to find safety, the man had pulled the boat up onto the bank until it was solidly out of the current, but he hadn't tied the line. The fisherman had then left the boat and their supplies, fishing equipment, a rifle, and an expensive watch. I hurried to the place where Old Paint had been abandoned. Wet grasses soaked me to the waist, and I was sure that the rising river had swept the john-boat away.

I stood in the darkness and listened to the roar of the swollen Big Piney; the water was 10 feet above normal. The rest of the countryside was silent, as though in fear of the angry river. That night I said good-bye to an old friend, for I knew the john-boat wouldn't survive the raging stream. The St. Louis man was heartbroken over the loss of his equipment, and left his address, in case anything might be recovered.

A week after the flood, a friend and I returned to the Piney in a newer boat. We floated the lower end; I suppose I hoped that some miracle might have spared Old Paint from the flood.

The river was down by then, but the water was still high enough for easy floating, and the fishing was good. But I still couldn't get Old Paint out of my mind. Nearly every stretch of water reminded me of things that had happened in the years of my boyhood; the place were I shot my first wood duck; the riffle where the big buck crossed the river in front of me two summers ago; an eddy where I camped and caught a big catfish on a trotline.

Suddenly, we arrived at the gravel bar where Dad, Charley, and I had swamped on the duck hunt nearly 10 years before. I glanced toward the willows where I had helped Dad and his cousin gather driftwood and leaves to build the life-saving fire on that cold December day.

Way back in the thick willows, I glimpsed a flash of green. I quickly reversed my paddle stroke, backing the boat to the bar. I plunged through the willows, and stopped below Old Paint.

The boat was perched on top of a 10-foot-high heap of debris. The bow of the john-boat pointed downstream as though the craft were ready and raring to float. I climbed onto the drift, and I was amazed to find all of the equipment that the St. Louis man had abandoned the week before during that stormy night. I could imagine how happy he would be to recover his gear. But he couldn't be any happier than I was.

That summer, I retired Old Paint to the eddy at the mouth of Hog Creek for limited use during the remainder of its days. The john-boat had lasted about twice as long as our other boats. Because of my sentimental attachment to Old Paint, the craft had been painted, patched, and treated with wood preservative each year since Dad had built it.

I have gone back to the eddy often, but Old Paint is now beyond much use for any rugged floating. Next spring, the high waters of the Piney will take the boat away, and the summer drifts along the river will contain pieces of the john-boat that has become a part of the Piney to me.

A boat is a boat, I guess — nothing more than boards and paint, and memories. Boards and paint are destined to rot away, but memories become priceless with age.

I'll remember my boyhood on the Big Piney, and a john-boat that we called Old Paint. And I guess that I'll just never feel completely comfortable in a canoe.

Chapter 3
The Big Deer Bet

Coach Wilkens came to Texas County when I was only 13 — he made an impression on me that will last forever.

The coach was a pretty fair pool shooter, and an educated man who could sit down and tell hunting stories with the best of the front bench regulars.

The front bench regulars were a dozen or so old-timers who had spent their lives hunting and fishing the Ozarks of southern Missouri. In their later years they spent time on the front bench of my father's pool hall, remembering.

It was a small country pool hall, the kind of place where a 13-year-old kid could fit right in. In fact, I ran the place much of the time. When I wasn't too busy, I liked to sit near the big front bench on my three-legged stool listening to Ol' Bill and Ol' Jim and Jess Wolf and Virgil Halstead and anyone else who wanted to tell tall stories about hunting and fishing in Big Piney River country.

Coach Wilkens fit in with the front bench regulars like a bow-tie salesman at a cockfight. But he was the only teacher I ever knew who came into the pool hall, and that alone made him my hero. My other teachers were constantly urging me to spend more time doing homework and less time in the pool hall. In fact, some went so far as to say that a 13-year-old boy shouldn't even be allowed in such a place.

Coach Wilkens didn't feel that way. He said there were lots of ways to be smart, and in their own way, Ol' Bill and old-timers like him had a lot to teach the world if only someone would listen.

It was something how the Coach earned a spot on that front bench, an outsider with an education, somehow accepted and appreciated for what he was. In time it was obvious that the old men liked Coach Wilkens, and he liked them.

In fact, he even went trotline fishing with Ol' Bill

one night during the summer, and Virgil Halstead let him go bow hunting on his back forty, even though all the front bench regulars hooted at the idea of a grown man out there chasin' deer with a bow and arrow.

There were some jaws that dropped a bit when Coach killed a forkhorn buck a half-dozen days into October. But deer season was deer season, not a time for playin' Indians, as Ol' Bill often said. And firearms deer season in the Ozarks took place in mid-November, when the bucks were in the rut and a man nearly froze to death before the first rays of sun hit the forest floor.

Coach Wilkens and Ol' Bill argued over that quite a bit. Coach said he figured the only thing easier than killing a deer during gun season was gigging fish in a rain barrel or maybe huntin' house cats with a shotgun.

Ol' Bill would never forget that. He propped one foot on the spittoon, and shifted his chaw of tobacco and ran a leathery hand over his stubble of beard.

"I didn't say it was hard to get a deer, young feller," he said with an air of indignation. "But some of us don't hunt a deer, we hunt them ol' vetern, thicket-sneakin', brush-huggin' rascals with antlers the size of ax handles."

All the front bench regulars laughed at that. Ol' Bill had pretty much put this upstart in his place. Everyone knew that Bill had taken some nice bucks. He was a good hunter, no question about that. He always got his deer, and it was usually a dandy with antlers that anyone would be proud to set over the fireplace.

Coach wasn't offended by such talk, he was smiling too, but there was a gleam in his eye as he answered old Bill's boast.

"Maybe things are different here in the Ozarks," he said. "Back in Ohio we had quite a few more big bucks."

Ol' Bill started to say something, but Coach wouldn't let him get a word in.

"I remember once when I was a kid how my dad bet some windbag deer hunter that he could get a better buck in three days than the other feller could get in a week."

Coach paused a minute, and Ol' Bill jumped in, "How much did he lose?"

"He didn't lose," Coach said, "and the name Wilkens still causes folks to think of big bucks back home. It grieved my poor ol' daddy somethin' terrible that I didn't carry on in his shoes, but I'd feel terrible betting with some ol' timer who had spent most of his life hunting bucks the size of billy goats."

Ol' Bill stood up to walk around the spittoon, and I knew the fur was about to fly. Unfortunately, I had to go rack up a back table and collect the money, and when I returned it was all over. Coach and Ol' Bill had $20 bet on who could bring in the best buck. Jess Wolf, Virgil Halstead and Ol' Jim were to be the judges. It wasn't a situation that favored the coach, but he didn't seem concerned. If he lost $20 he could afford it, and the whole thing was a whole lot of fun for him.

Ol' Bill didn't have that kind of attitude. He meant to take Coach Wilkens' money with no mercy shown.

News of the bet spread around town like wildfire over the next few days. Most of the front bench regulars were of the opinion that coach had lost his money. Ol' Bill was more than just a good story teller, he was an honest-to-goodness outdoorsman with more big bucks to his credit than any hunter in the county.

Back in the days when there were hardly any deer in the Ozarks, just after they opened a limited season, Bill would bring bucks to the check station that would attract bigger crowds than a parade.

My Grandpa Dablemont told me all about that, but he told me, too, that Ol' Bill wasn't able to hunt the Ozarks hills as he once did. Grandpa and Ol' Bill were trapping partners in years past and my granddad was one of his closest friends. Sometimes when Bill would be telling a big story about hunting or fishing, he'd point to my grandpa there on the front bench and say, "Ain't that the way it was, Fred?"

Of course Grandpa would smile and nod his head and come back with another story.

When we were fishing for black perch one afternoon on Brushy Creek, I asked my granddad if all those stories were gospel truth. "In a gen'ral sorta way, I reckon," he answered. "Sometimes as the years roll on, fish get a mite bigger and antlers get a bit wider."

Grandpa stared awhile at the bobber sitting stone-still on the surface, and he told me something I'd always remember.

"Ol' men like me an' Bill come to a time when they can't do what they once could," he said. "Then all they got left is mem'ries an' stories to make 'em feel a bit younger an' more important in the eyes of a young sprout like you. Don't begrudge 'em that boy, it's all they got left to keep 'em goin'."

Still and all, I couldn't help but pull for Coach. Ol' Bill was just doing too much blowing and bragging about how he had that bet won. I couldn't see it at the time, but Ol' Bill wanted to sound a good deal more confident than he was.

It started showing a little, though, just before the deer season opened. Ol' Bill mentioned on occasion that one leg was giving him problems, and he wasn't going to be able to hunt his old territory. Then he went on something terrible about how there were so many greenhorns from the city these days that they were spooking the big, older bucks into heavy cover, making night dwellers out of them.

Bill would have been seriously worried if he knew about Coach's grandmother's farm. It wasn't big, but it joined my Grandpa McNew's farm and there were several deer that crossed back and forth between the farms. Along one wooded ridge there was a natural passageway from one farm to another, with the kind of heavy vegetation that gave big bucks the security they needed. Coach had a stand built there, and it was a good one. By bow hunting in October, he had the advantage over Bill. There were two or three bucks using that ridge that were real eye-poppers. I didn't see them, but Coach showed me their tracks and told me all about them.

One afternoon in November, he showed me the fresh scrapes near his tree platform.

"This is where I'll be hunting," he told me. "You're welcome to use the one I've got built over next to your granddad's farm. The same buck that made these scrapes probably made one or two over that way, I would suppose."

As I remember it, the opening day of deer season that year dawned cold and clear and still, close to perfect if it hadn't been so cold. When you're 13 years old, its tough to sit in a tree stand very long, and 30 degrees makes it next to impossible.

That's all compounded by the fact that 13-year-old boys rarely have much confidence — at least I didn't. I had never killed a deer, and I didn't figure I ever would.

Nevertheless, I may have played a part in Coach Wilkens' success because when I climbed down from my stand just hours after I climbed into it, I heard a deer snort, then two. I never saw them, but the deer turned back toward the Coach and it wasn't 10 minutes later that three does trotted past him.

It's a wonder how smart bucks are most of the time. The big ones are harder to find than chiggers on a redbone hound. But during the rut, bucks aren't normal, and behind those three does, a hundred yards or so, was an eight-point buck that some men hunt for a lifetime.

I heard Coach shoot when I was almost to my grandmother's farmhouse — the first report followed by a second — the two shots only four or five seconds apart.

Coach was back at my grandparents' house in 30 minutes. The buck had been hit hard, then turned back toward my stand, and had crossed onto my grandparent's property. When he discovered I wasn't on my stand, Coach returned to his pickup and came to ask permission to trail the buck on neighboring land. It was permission he didn't need, of course, but Coach was ahead of his time during that era in the Ozarks.

I went along to help find the buck, the excitement building as Coach described the deer, at least an eight-pointer he figured, one of the two big bucks he had seen before.

If I had stayed on the stand, I probably would have seen the wounded buck pass by me within 80 yards or so. The blood trail was easy to follow; in a few minutes we trailed the buck into a cedar thicket where he had gone down for good.

I knew at first glance that Coach had won his bet with Ol' Bill. Not that it was any kind of record or anything, but the antlers were wide and heavy, well-proportioned with eight strong points, maybe a ninth projecting low off the left beam just over the forehead.

As Ozarks bucks go, it was a good one. Most any hunter would have wanted that set of antlers to hang over his fireplace or front porch. It was the kind of buck that most of the front bench regulars would remember in years to come, a little bigger after each season added some glory to the memory.

Coach field-dressed the buck, and I watched and helped and went on something awful about how I couldn't wait to see the look on Ol' Bill's face that night. As I remember it, Coach was elated with that buck.

But later, Coach seemed more subdued. On the way in to the check station, he asked me if I reckoned Ol' Bill had ever killed a buck that big. Of course he had, and several at that. I told Coach about pictures of big bucks in my grandpa's album.

"Ol' Bill has probably hung as many big bucks in the smoke house as any hunter in the county," I told him.

As the pickup bounced over the gravel road toward town, I said something that caused Coach Wilkens to become quiet and somber.

"Ol' Bill is gonna lose more than just $20 because of this here buck," I told him cheerily. "This might stop all his bragging about being the best deer hunter in Texas County."

We stopped at the pool hall late in the morning. No one had seen Ol' Bill, but several of the front bench regulars were there and everyone pretty much agreed that this buck made Coach a winner.

"He'll likely not bag one at all now," Jess Wolf said of his old friend. "Ol' Bill ain't likely to bring in a buck smaller'n that'n, an' he ain't apt to see a better one."

I don't rightly remember how I spent the afternoon, but I was there in the pool hall that evening. I took over while my dad went home for supper. It was a busy Saturday evening, as always on opening day of deer season. Several hunters were anxious to tell about bucks they had bagged or missed. A few others talked about the one they only saw. But the conversation eventually got around to the nice eight-pointer that hung in Coach Wilkens' garage that night.

Though subdued, Ol' Bill was not ready to surrender. He said he hadn't seen the big buck that everyone claimed Coach had killed, but he figured he had passed up one bigger that very morning.

There were a few chuckles and Ol' Bill even grinned a little as he cut off a plug of tobacco.

"I'll say this for that Coach feller," Bill went on, "He's a dang poor deer hunter if he ain't down here braggin' about it."

While everyone laughed I went to answer the phone. It was Coach Wilkens, and he wanted to know if I had said anything about helping him find his buck. I told him I had tried several times, but a 13-year-old kid sometimes has trouble getting a word in edgewise. Coach told me that what he was about to do would seem a bit strange to me, but he'd explain things later.

I don't guess anything ever puzzled me more — especially when Coach walked in and acted like he had bent the barrel on his best deer rifle. You've never seen such a long face on a man that was so happy only eight or nine hours before. Amid all the congratulations and backslapping, Coach just reached in his pocket, pulled out a $20 bill and handed it to Ol' Bill. It grew quiet in the pool hall and Ol' Bill nearly swallowed his tobacco. He had come to the pool hall ready to eat crow and try to hang on to his dignity for awhile, hoping for a miracle later in the week. But everyone in that pool hall thought Ol' Bill had given up any hope of winning the bet.

Coach sat down on the front bench, and the snooker game on the front table stopped for awhile as he explained why he had decided to concede. I couldn't believe what I was hearing.

"It was Friday evening just after school," he said. "I was on my way over to Edgar Springs to see about a rifle a fellow had for sale, when two does jumped out in the highway and crossed in front of me. I slowed down a bit and some salesman from St. Louis came roarin' 'round me doing about 60. About that time, a big buck came across the ditch behind those two does and that salesman slammed on his brakes hard.

"Well the darn fool was a little late, and he hit that buck just hard enough to roll him a time or two. For a moment or so, I thought the buck wasn't hurt bad, but then I saw he was having a hard time climbing the embankment going up into the woods, one leg broke for sure."

Everyone was really caught up in the story, and Coach acted like he'd rather kiss the local librarian than confess to what he did.

"Well to make a long story short, I helped the St. Louis feller look over his car, and he went on with little more than a bent fender. I bought that rifle, and on the way back I stopped to see if that buck had made it very far."

Coach paused for a moment, shook his head and stared at the floor.

"He hadn't," he said sadly. "So I put him out of his misery and called the game warden, and he said the situation being what it was he didn't see why I couldn't dress him out, hang him up and go back this morning and put my tag on him, so that's what I did. But it isn't right to claim some crippled buck as a trophy, and I'm here to pay up."

I stood there listening with my mouth open, knowing better than to protest, but wishing more than anything that I could say something.

The front bench regulars admitted that some of the local hunters might have never owned up to such a thing, but it was admirable of a man to not let good venison go to waste. Coach had done an unselfish thing, sacrificing his deer tag and telling the truth even if it cost him $20.

Ol' Bill wouldn't take the money, though. He said that before he could win it fair and square, he'd have to bring in a buck of his own. He said Coach should keep his fingers crossed, but with the rest of the week left, his chances weren't good.

In school on Monday, Coach explained everything. "It was a dumb thing I did, Larry," he told me. "I caused Ol' Bill to put more than $20 on the line. He was betting his self-worth, his stature in the eyes of his friends. If I had won that bet, that old man would have lost the thing that meant the most to him — his reputation as a deer hunter."

I told him I understood, and I would help him keep his secret.

"Everyone deserves to have something he can brag about when he grows old," Coach told me. "I'm not ever going to forget that again."

Coach couldn't have stood taller in my eyes than he did right then. And I suppose if it had ended that way, I would have had quite a story to tell someday. But it didn't end there, because on Wednesday morning Ol' Bill drove his battered old red International pickup into town with a buck in the back of it. For two or three hours, folks gathered along Main Street to look at what Jess Wolf said was the "the derndest set of horns I ever seen."

It was an atypical set of antlers that had two long tines growing straight down, and others sticking up and out like thorns on a honey locust tree. Some said it had 14 points; some said it had better than 20. I was in school so I never saw it, except for the pictures.

Ol' Bill and his three judges made a big thing of taking Coach's $20 the following Saturday night with all the front bench regulars there looking on.

Coach looked awful humble, but I knew he was enjoying himself. He had more friends in that pool hall that night than any Northerner had a right to expect.

But at the right time, Ol' Bill sat down and propped his feet on a spittoon and told Coach he wasn't much of a liar.

"Half a dozen fellers I know that saw your buck said he didn't have no broke leg," Bill grinned. "An', boy, we all know the game warden roun' here."

Before long, Coach sheepishly admitted he had made the whole thing up and there was a good deal of knee-slapping and ribbing going on.

Bill said he was gonna forgive him for all that. "It's a good thing I didn't believe that story though, or it woulda ruint my whole dad-blame deer season."

Coach looked at Ol' Bill with question marks all over his face. "How could I..."

Bill didn't let him finish. "If I'd a believed that yarn of yours," he said as he shifted his tobacco, "I'd a shot me a six-pointer on Monday mornin'!"

I don't know, it could be that Ol' Bill had his most memorable deer season because he was so intent on winning that $20 bet fair and square. But I doubt he passed up a six-pointer. The front bench regulars were still talking about both bucks in late winter. Coach came in once or twice a week to argue with Ol' Bill about what made the best coonhound or what shot size was best for duck hunting.

Just before spring, they really got carried away over who was the best river fisherman and before it was over, Coach and Bill had bet $20 on who could catch the biggest brownie before July. Ol' Jim, Jess Wolf and Virgil Halstead were to be the judges. I don't think Coach would have had it any other way.

Chapter 4
FARGO

My cousins and I hunted everything: rabbits, coons, possums, squirrels, even bullfrogs. And we bagged our share of quail when they'd jump up in the open, fly straight and stay out of the brush. Most of them didn't, though, and we learned in time that quail hunting was a rich man's sport just like Uncle Rob said it was. Shells cost seven or eight cents each and if you figured it up, one quail could cost you anywhere from a buck and a half to two dollars. In comparison, a possum would cost about seven or eight cents, and a squirrel only twice that at the most. A rabbit might cost a little more, but not if he was sitting. None of us ever saw a quail sitting when we were hunting, and I hate to think of what might have happened if we had.

With quail, it was always the same, up and gone in the blink of an eyelash, and nothing to show for it but empty shotshell hulls.

Uncle Rob said that to hunt quail right, you needed a quail dog, and to get one you'd need quite a bit of money. We ranged in age from 14 to 16, and if you combined all the money the four of us had, you couldn't have come up with enough to rescue some poor mutt from the dog pound. But one night in the early fall of 1962, divine providence smiled upon us, and for the cost of two gallons of gas we became the proud owners of a professional bird dog.

We headed for the Horseshoe Bend river-bottoms that night in my dad's 1949 pick-up, with two gallons of gas in the tank and one of the Floyd boys in the back with his grandfather's coonhound. In addition to Rupert Floyd and his dog, there was me and my cousin Buck, whose real name was Arlin, even though he had never been safely called that by anyone but his mother. And then there was Buck's younger brother Andy and our other cousin De-Wayne, with the emphasis on the "De."

We were on our way home that night about 10:30 or 11:00, completely empty handed, when he appeared in the road before us, as if he had decided to end it all, and chose our pick-up to throw himself in front of. I hit the brake, and Rupert and DeWayne, who were riding in the back with the coon dog, nearly went over the top of the cab.

In our path sat a half-starved liver and white pointer, a genuine bird dog, long limbed, square-headed and lost. We knew what he was from the smoke-stained picture in the pool hall, the one that showed the two dogs locked on point. He had an old beat-up leather collar around his neck, and the name Fargo on a metal tag. But there was nothing else.

For Fargo, life was about to take a turn for the better. That fall night, Andy climbed into the back with Rupert and DeWayne, and gave the scrawny old pointer his spot on the front seat between me and Buck. The dog sat there and looked out the window like he had done it all his life.

Buck and I were thinking the same thing...a stroke of pure luck had brought us a professional bird dog.

That night, old Fargo had a late supper, probably the best one he had seen in many a day. It consisted of a half-dozen cold biscuits that Buck and I found on Aunt Mollie's dinner table well past midnight, after everyone had long been asleep. We put the big pointer up in a small shed just off the barn, and hoped to the almighty he wouldn't howl. He didn't!

Early the next morning we got a good look at our new bird dog in broad daylight. He left his bed of straw with reluctance, rising to tiptoe out into the morning sunshine like an old-timer looking for that first cup of coffee.

Cousin DeWayne had brought a bag of table scraps that morning and they disappeared in the blink of an eye, along with part of the bag. We headed for the farmhouse to show Uncle Rob our new dog, hoping he'd tell us it was a sure-enough bird dog. Uncle Rob stood back and took a long, hard look, scratching a days worth of stubble with one hand, the other thrust deep in the pocket of his bib overalls.

First he looked at Fargo's teeth and took note that part of one ear was gone. He allowed as how we sure enough had found a genuine bird dog all right, an English pointer from start to finish and he was a great deal closer to the finish than the start.

"I reckon he's pretty near as old as you boys," Uncle Rob told us, "but that ain't all bad. Age means experience, and that's mighty valuable to a bird dog...experience."

We looked from one to another, each face beaming with expectation. If old Fargo hadn't had any recent experience, he was about to get some.

We headed for the back forty before noon, me and DeWayne and Buck. In the early fall there had been one good-sized covey there, about 20 birds or so. We had hunted them hard and there were only 18 or 19 birds left.

Fargo saw those shotguns and you could see he was familiar with the pastime of bird hunting. He ranged before us, behind us and beside us, looking for quail with intensity. Ol' Fargo the pointer was a veteran of many fall hunts — you could see that. We weren't 20 minutes from the pick-up when he froze up, still as a statue, just like the dog in the picture at the pool hall. For me and Buck and DeWayne it was the first time we had seen a dog on point, and there was magic in it. We snuck in behind him, slow and cautious, not wanting to see it come to an end too quickly.

Before we were ready, a cottontail bounded out of a briar patch nearby, and the three shotguns roared in semi-unison. It wasn't unusual for that to happen when we hunted together, and it wasn't unusual for all of us to miss. Chances are good that two of us missed the rabbit that day, but one of us didn't, and a celebration followed.

Old Fargo wouldn't retrieve the rabbit, he just nudged it with his nose. But as Buck said, you don't need a dog to bring you a rabbit that's already dead. If he finds it and points it, what more could anyone ask for? We didn't know then that bird dogs weren't suppose to point rabbits. If we had been told such a thing, we would have found it hard to accept. A rabbit was a far greater prize than a quail simply because it was so much larger. Three rabbits made a good meal for a family, and we had no idea how many quail it would take to feed a farm family because we had never bagged that many.

We felt sure that would change with old Fargo at our side. Over the next week or so, despite the annoyance of so many hours devoted to school, we got into two or three coveys of quail and I believe I could take you today and show you the three places where Fargo pointed singles from those coveys. It's true he didn't point the majority of them, but a dog can't be everywhere at once. Andy and Buck and DeWayne and I didn't sit around and wait for Fargo to find everything, we got in there with him and beat the brush. The old dog pointed one covey late in the evening as we hunted after school, and it was a thing of beauty. But he eased in a bit closer, and just as he was comfortable, the quail flushed wild, a good 10 feet away. Uncle Rob said they'd do that on occasion when they'd been hard hunted, and Lord knows those quail were hard hunted by us boys. We flushed those birds so many times they had a half inch wore off their wing tips.

Aunt Mollie was a good woman, and Uncle Rob said many a time it was hard to be married to a good woman and get along in the world. It wasn't much easier having a good woman for a mother. Of course DeWayne and I had similar mothers, so we understood.

During the summer, they near about worked us boys to death, making us snap beans, hoe the garden and pick blackberries and seeing to it we were in Sunday School on one of the only two mornings of the week we could fish. In the winter time, it didn't get much better, with wood-chopping and homework and regular bathing when there wasn't hardly time for it. But what got all of us boys a bit out of sorts from time to time was the insistence that we were apt to turn out worse than our dads, and the constant lectures about honesty and idle hands and grades a good two notches above what was normal.

Uncle Rob said we could learn from it, but he said no one ever did. He figured we'd wind up married some day, watching our own sons get the same type of treatment. But nobody figured on honesty being carried to such great heights that we'd have to run a newspaper ad telling the whole world we had found a great bird dog and would like to give him back to whoever was stupid enough to have lost him.

But that's what Aunt Mollie did one day while Uncle Rob was at the sale barn and us boys were in school and there wasn' t a level headed soul to stop her. And she didn't just put in there that we had a lost dog. No sir, she said we had a brown and white pointer named Fargo and told where it could be found right down to the last detail.

We clung to the faint hope that Fargo's owner had died, or maybe would die before he got to Uncle Rob's farm. But that kind of thing only happens in the movies. On Saturday morning, as Andy and Buck and I helped unload firewood, looking forward to going hunting just as soon as we could, here came an old rusty DeSoto up the drive. The driver was a shifty-looking, cigar-smoking character who was so fat he could barely get out of the car, let alone hunt quail. Fargo sat there and looked befuddled, and it was plain to all of us that he hadn't ever seen the guy before either.

Uncle Rob shook his hand and was so nice it would have made you about half sick just to see it. Every one of us boys were hopin' he'd meet the guy with the same kind of resistance he'd shown to that encyclopedia salesman a few months back. But he acted like any time he might invite the shyster in for coffee. And I reckoned in the back of my mind he had caved in to Aunt Mollie and was fixin' to give away the only bird-dog we had ever found.

He called old Fargo over, and the guy looked him over good and said sure enough that was his brother-in-law's dog, and he'd see to it that old Fargo got back to his rightful owner. Uncle Rob looked so relieved I guess he didn't see the tears in our eyes — 15- and 16-year old boys who wouldn't cry if you pulled out our toe-nails, just about to break down and blubber.

But then a funny thing happened. Uncle Rob went to shakin' that ol' boys hand and talkin' about what a great relief this was, and he turned and told Buck to go call the widow Foster to tell her we had found the owner of the dog and she could come down and settle up with him right there.

None of us had no idea what he was talkin' about, but before we could ask questions, Uncle Rob turned to the man and said he had took about all the abuse from that neighbor lady he intended to take. Her with the sheriff out there two or three times and tryin' to get him to pay for those chickens and the goose and those little pigs. He said he didn't argue that old Fargo had kilt the chickens and the goose, but he didn't know about the pigs, and she should have built the pens stronger in the first place.

"I told the sheriff when he was out here the last time that I thought a hunnert dollars was too danged much," Uncle Rob lamented, "but if we hadn't found his owner, I b'lieve I'da had to pay up, with that lawyer a her'n getting' into things the way he was. Now I reckon she can't lay no fault off on me an' the boys, since we've got proof it ain't our dog."

With that, the fat man nearly choked on his cigar, and he circled old Fargo, giving him a new look while Uncle Rob went on, telling Buck to hurry that call and tell the widow if she wanted her money to get down there pronto.

Buck had figured it out by then and he was on his way to the house while the visitor crawfished about that dog. He said he'd need to be sure about the pointer, maybe he'd get his brother-in-law out there real soon to take care of the details. Then he said he didn't know if there'd be room for a dog in that DeSoto and he was in it and gone almost before the screen door slammed behind Buck. As the dust settled along that gravel road, there was whooping and hollering and backslapping of significant magnitude, enough so that Aunt Mollie came out to see what was going on.

Uncle Rob told her we were just happy because we thought there was a good chance Fargo's rightful owner would be coming soon to take the dog home, and he told her how the man in the DeSoto was his brother-in-law, and how there might be a reward in it for us. We all worked hard to keep a straight face when Aunt Mollie commented as she returned to the house on how proud she was of Uncle Rob showing us boys that indeed honesty had its rewards.

It was the last claim made to the aging pointer, and even Aunt Mollie agreed, finally, that he was our dog. We all forgave her in time.

For a couple more years, we hunted with Fargo without really making a dent in the area quail population. But he did eventually catch one of the widow Foster's banty roosters, and he fell in love with her pretty little collie bitch shortly afterward. I think the widow was less affected by the loss of the banty, which we paid for, than the litter of half-pointer pups we had to find homes for.

Buck joined the army out of high school, and DeWayne went into the Navy. Andy got a good job and a wife, I went to college, and old Fargo retired on Aunt Mollie's front porch to retrieve an occasional mole or mouse. For the most part, everything went pretty much like Uncle Rob said it would, as we all wound up married to good women, who would give away our best dog at the drop of a hat. But every last one of us are still quail hunters and the last time I saw Buck he had big old male pointer he said was a real cracker-jack. He said he called him Fargo.

Chapter 5
Old Fighter

The river was quiet. An owl had been calling earlier in the evening, but now it was close to midnight and he had stopped. Occasionally, a big bullfrog downstream broke the stillness with a series of bellows, then again there was only the constant rushing of water over a nearby shoal.

Wrapped in quilts, I lay beneath a makeshift lean-to made of a big brown tarpaulin that kept off the dew but not the chill of the early summer night.

Next to me, Grandpa was snoring softly. Hollowed-out beds on gravelbars would never be as comfortable for me as they were for him. His 63 years of life on the river had accustomed him to that sort of thing. It was June, 1961, and I was 13 years old — about to enter my first year of high school. I wasn't much interested in English literature or math or history, but I was intent upon learning the important things in life, like how to build a john-boat, run a rough shoal, or set trotlines to catch big catfish.

I had good teachers. My dad and granddad spent most of their spare time on the Piney with me. We hunted the river in the fall and we always went fishing in the summer. Dad preferred to tempt smallmouth and goggle-eye (rock bass) with artificial lures, but Grandpa was a trotline fisherman. We went after big flathead catfish at every opportunity. I lay there watching the sky light up occasionally from a distant thunderstorm and thinking about the other trips we had taken that summer. Finally, I got up to gather some wood.

The campfire that had been burning so well only an hour before now lay in orange embers with faint blue around the charred logs. Sparks leaped high as I rekindled the fire. There was no reason to go back to sleep now.

I sat down beside the fire and moved the coffee pot a little closer. The flames began to grow again, gradually illuminating a small area of the gravelbar.

I poured a cup of coffee as Grandpa continued to

snore. Soon that built-in alarm clock of his would awaken him and we would run the trotlines. I could picture a 20-pound flathead lashing with every ounce of his strength against one of our lines.

It was a good night for trotlining. Occasionally, distant lightning would silhouette the southern Missouri hills against the sky, and rumbles of thunder, muffled by distance, would follow.

Grandpa had said it would storm some before dawn, and he was usually right. To him, a storm pretty nearly guaranteed that he'd get a big catfish.

As the coffee chased away the chill, Grandpa stirred, then got up and joined me at the fire.

He filled and lighted the carbide lamps as he downed a cup of coffee. Such lamps were tools of the trade for the old-time trotline fisherman. The lamps are a simple means of providing light, and they leave the hands free. They are the same type as those that miners once wore mounted on their caps by a special frame. A lower cup is filled with carbide, and an upper compartment is filled with water. As the water drips slowly to the lower cup, an acetylene gas is formed. The light from the flame that is fed by the gas is directed by a four- to-six-inch reflector, softly lighting a large area. The lamps were a part of trotlining as Grandpa knew it, and he refused to change.

The river looks somber in the light of a carbide lamp, like you might imagine it looked at the dawn of man when mammoths walked the earth. The mist that rose from the water, the silence and the chill set an eerie mood. We switched our bait from the boat's built-in live-box to a bucket and then pushed off in the john-boat to check and rebait the lines.

I watched our campfire disappear around the bend behind us as I listened to the slurp of Grandpa's paddle blade entering and leaving the water. Grandpa pushed our boat forward into the deep water of the Ginseng eddy. The Ginseng is a big, deep eddy on the upper Big Piney at the point where the river is closest to Houston, Missouri, only five or six miles away. It was one of a dozen or so eddies on the river that he favored.

As we prepared to run our lines, a whippoorwill began to call.

Trotlines are not easy to set, and it takes a lot of experience to learn how and where to set them. The best places to set trotlines are in the deepest eddies — quiet water with big rocks, ledges or bluffs beneath which big flatheads of 20 to 30 pounds find a place to hide.

The main line is tied from one bank to the other and is stretched fairly tight. Big catfish hooks are attached to the main line with nylon strings or dropper lines about 15 inches long. Hooks must be three feet apart, and knots in the main line keep the dropper lines and hooks from sliding and becoming entangled. Rock weights of about fist-size are tied on after every fourth hook to carry the line to the bottom where the flatheads lurk. It's a rugged sport — and a dangerous one. Heavy lines must be handled with care. Many anglers have become entangled in weighted trotlines and drowned.

Grandpa found the first line along the bank and lifted it with his paddle blade for me to take. As we moved along the line toward the deeper water, I felt the trotline surging in my hand, and I imagined a catfish just ahead.

Finally the fish surfaced only a short distance away, and I glimpsed a big brown body in the glow of the carbide lamp. Grandpa maneuvered the boat and gave advice as I excitedly hauled in the big fish.

Grandpa whistled softly as I laid the big fish in the bottom of the boat. It wasn't a catfish; it was a giant smallmouth bass, somewhere around six pounds.

Everyone around knew of this particular fish — Old Fighter, the smallmouth that had earned a reputation as King of the Ginseng eddy. But until now he'd never been boated. I looked at him for awhile. He was by far the biggest smallmouth I'd ever seen.

My father was one of the many fishermen who had hooked and lost this big bass. Dad and I floated the river often, trying to catch big smallmouth on lures. I had seen Dad catch big bronzebacks on artificial lures, and — fishing the Big Piney by myself — I had caught several two- to-three-pounders on minnows and nightcrawlers. But never had I dreamed of catching a fish like Old Fighter.

Bass aren't usually caught on a trotline, especially with bait as large as Grandpa liked to use. Grandpa baited his lines with big chubs and suckers six to 10 inches long, and with doughgut minnows, otherwise known as stonerollers. These aren't as attractive to bass as they are to catfish, but we had used a few longear sunfish, and the enormous smallmouth had taken a liking to one of them.

Old Fighter's dark brown body, broad and deep, glistened in the lamplight as he lay in the bottom of the boat. Even in defeat, the bright red eye that faced up blazed defiantly.

"Old Fighter himself," Grandpa said. "Thought I'd never see the day he'd leave this river. Maybe we oughta turn 'im loose, seein' as how we was after catfish anyway."

Immediately I protested.

"It's not against the law; so why shouldn't I keep him?"

"No reason a'tall," Grandpa answered as he began to rebait the trotline. "He's yours, an' a fine trophy."

Reassured, I laid the bronzeback in the live-box. The fish was nearly too big for the well and when he felt water again, he furiously sought freedom. But finally he lay there on his side in resignation, his tail bent upward out of the water.

As Grandpa hooked minnows to the hooks along the trotline, I watched the fish, slowly moving his gills from time to time but otherwise motionless.

"I'll see if Dad will have him mounted," I said. "Then I'll have him forever."

The old man across the boat from me reached for another minnow as the t rumble of thunder drowned out the whippoorwill's call.

"They was a time," he said, "when I thought big smallmouth would live forever in these Ozarks rivers. That was years ago, before they began to cut the trees along the Big Piney and water cattle on the shoals. An' it was before they hauled gravel out for cement, an' let the silt an' mud yellow the water an' fill the eddies."

He paused to bend a straightened hook, then peered

into the minnow bucket, looking for a big doughgut.

"There was lots of Old Fighters when I was a boy."

In the light of the headlamp Grandpa hooked another big minnow through the lips. "We oughta have a big flathead on this'n come mornin'. Specially if that thunderhead moves on over this way."

"Grandpa," I said, still thinking about the big smallmouth, "do you think there's any more like him in the Piney?"

"I don't reckon," he replied. "Fact is, they prob'ly ain't many left half his size. But I guess they'd not get much bigger anyway if folks get the dam in they been wantin'.

"I hear tell the dam would mean lots more money for everybody," he continued. "I can't figger why the brown bass an' the mink an' kingfishers and such things ain't worth nothin' to nobody."

Grandpa baited the last hook, then lifted the line to see that it wasn't hung up on anything. Finally he dropped the trotline, and we watched it sink from sight into the depths of the Ginseng. Then he picked up the paddle and headed slowly back upstream toward camp.

"You know, boy," he said quietly, "I guess me an' that old bass got a lot in common. He's prob'ly layin' in the live-box thinkin' over his life, bein' thankful he lived when the rivers ran clear and free, 'fore folks knowed about dams an' lakes and such. I 'spect he's obliged he lived when he did, 'cause he knows the world is a-changin' an' there ain't gonna be a place for him much longer. An' when I look back an' remember all the happy days an' nights I've spent along these ol' river bluffs, I kinda understand how he feels. Maybe a little sad, but mostly mighty thankful for gettin' to be what he was."

We moved closer to camp against the current, and I noticed that with the coming of the storm things were getting quiet. Lightning suddenly silhouetted the riverbanks again, and close behind the flash, thunder rolled — louder now. I knew we'd be moving our beds and equipment to the big cave along the bluff behind the gravelbar for the rest of the night. Despite the approaching storm, I felt secure just knowing the cave was there.

Then I reached inside the live-well and grasped the big bass by the lower jaw, lifting him high so I could see him close up.

"We're after catfish," I said finally, lowering the bass into the water beside the boat, "not bass."

Together Grandpa and I watched the big bass. He lay motionless in the quiet water for a moment, as though uncertain of his freedom. Suddenly, with a powerful sweep of his tail, he shot away in the direction of the Ginseng eddy, where he would continue for awhile to rule the dark, quiet water beneath the great white bluff.

The Ginseng eddy is still there. The old bluff looks much the way it did then, though big hunks of algae now float along the river during the summer...something we never saw back then.

Other eddies that I once trotlined can be waded now. There are stumps where century-old sycamores shaded the Big Piney of the past, and just below the Ginseng eddy a landowner recently bulldozed the trees from a long stretch along the stream. The rumored dam didn't materialize, though the possibility of one is still mentioned from time to time.

But in my memory lingers that streak of brown moving away in the dim light of my carbide lamp. They are gone now — my grandfather and the big smallmouth. The Big Piney that they knew is gone, too.

Each year the Big Piney watershed deteriorates. Miles of the stream and its tributaries are cleared and bulldozed, and ever increasing numbers of cattle are allowed to erode the banks. Smallmouth hang on... smaller now and fewer in number... but still there. May they always be!

Chapter 6
The Blizzard on Netley Marsh

N etley Marsh lies at the tip of Lake Winnipeg, 10 or 12 square miles of grassy wetlands connected by creek channels and filled with waterfowl much of the year. When the wind blows from the south it pushes the water to the north, making the shallows even shallower. At times like that, the marsh is a kitten, but when the gales blow from the north, the tides from the giant lake push in quickly to raise the marsh as much as eight or 10 feet.

Scores of duck-hunters have died there over the last century. Most of those deaths occurred when waterfowlers left their boats to wade out and hunt in the grassy potholes and were caught by the north winds which raised the water and carried away the boats. For that reason, you pay attention to the wind and stay near your boat. We were paying attention that afternoon, 15 years ago, when the day came in like a lamb and slowly became a raging lion. At dawn John and Darrell and I were hunting geese in a Manitoba grain field. The hunting had been good and the three of us had killed a limit of 15 Canadas by 10 a.m.

We left the geese at a waterfowl-dressing business in nearby Balmoral, then ate quickly at a local cafe. Just a little after noon we hooked onto my duck-boat at our cabin on Netley Creek and backed it down the ramp for a few hours of duck hunting before heading back home the following day. We had already spent two mornings on the marsh and the duck hunting had been good. But there was a front moving in, snow predicted during the night, and it wouldn't hurt to have one last hunt before it arrived. We motored down the creek and into the Red River, then crossed the big, wide bay to a small channel which entered the marsh.

In the first hour we had a few ducks come in, but not many. It was about then we began to feel the cool air moving in, and with it, low gray clouds riding the new north wind. High in those clouds were strings of ducks, flock after flock, horizon-to-horizon in numbers which I have never seen before or since. Sailing southward on a strong wind, the ducks were leaving the northern prairies and potholes. The long fall migration was underway.

We watched it for awhile, a general uneasiness developing with the cold wind and the magnitude of the migration.

As we picked up our decoys there were the first few flecks of snow, and the light-hearted bantering we enjoy amongst ourselves had ceased. We were quiet, almost grim, watching those continuing masses of ducks moving over the wetlands, and the wind that had sprung from the north with a whisper had grown to bend the reeds over the marsh with a steady, low roar.

We knew what the bay would look like, but we had to cross it to reach the river channel to the southwest and our cabin. We were each in our early 30s then, with years of hunting experience, but when we broke from the small wind-whipped channel to the open bay, none of us had ever seen anything like that. Swells driven by the north wind were crashing across the open water six or eight feet high, and trying to cross the bay would have been suicide. We were trapped in the teeth of a Canadian norther and as we watched, the far bank, a mile away, faded into a white haze of driven snow.

The east-west channel we were on was well protected by a high bank of perhaps four or five-feet and then the high reeds to provide some protection from the wind. We chose a spot where a small bunch of woody shrubs also grew up above the reeds, and prepared to wait it out.

My duck boat was made for big water, 18 feet in length with a six-foot beam and a new 60-horse Evinrude motor. We secured it against the bank using the base of the bushes and stakes and ropes from the portable duck blind I use, knowing the water would rise and we could adjust for it. But when it rose high enough, there would be no way to stay out of that gale.

We emptied the decoys in the boat and filled the bags with marsh grasses, then removed a two-foot by six-foot, half-inch plywood cover which covers the back bench and the fuel tanks and batteries. John continued to cut grass and stuff it into the bags. We would spend the night, if we had to, on those soft and insulating bags of grass. Meanwhile, Darrell and I worked to make a roof over a section of the boat which would keep the snow and wind off of us. We set it up over the steering console to the front deck of my boat, and used metal poles from the duck blind, secured as solidly as possible with ropes and duct tape.

We were putting all our energy into those preparations, and I remember thinking that this all might be fun if it weren't for the raw fear we were all feeling deep in our gut.

The snow came in small, hard pellets mixed with wetter flakes. It would drive down for a while, then stop, then blast us again. The plywood made a roof above us, low, but high enough to crouch beneath. We used the camouflage material to enclose the three sides toward the wind.

For years I have used the weatherproof material made by a southern company called "Hide-em Hunter Specialties." I have two 20-foot sections and two 10-foot sections, and we doubled it to make a very protective wall around us. But again, we were down beneath the protective bank, and when the water rose enough, that makeshift cover would never stand against the open wind. It was just a matter of time. But there was hope that sometime during the night, the storm would abate; in the meantime we could rest there and stay warm and maybe even nap a little.

We would, indeed, combat the cold. All of us had heavy coveralls and masks and gloves and even heavy float coats to go over that. I shed my chest waders and pulled on leather boots I had brought along in a storage compartment.

John and Darrell had only their chest waders, but we had some extra dry socks from that compartment and in the dwindling light, they put them on.

My duck boat's emergency compartment holds stuff I always figure I'll never need — things like duct tape and extra rope, extra socks and gloves and stocking caps in waterproof bags. There's a can of charcoal starter fluid and an old flashlight which never works because the batteries are always dead. And all those things are there because at one time or another, I have had need for them, hunting ducks on various waters in the Midwest. But I never thought there would ever be a situation like we were in that night on Netley Marsh.

The real ace in the hole was a metal five-gallon bucket which always sits under the console with about four or five inches of sand in the bottom. All through December and into January, when the cold gets tough to handle in the Midwest and the duck-hunting is good, that bucket and a quarter of a sack of charcoal is all you need to have some warmth in case you get wet or your hands get numb with cold.

It just happened, and maybe it was something of a miracle, that we had stopped in a small town on the Iowa-South Dakota border and bought several boxes of groceries for our hunting trip to save money because the price of food is so much higher in Canada. I spotted a stack of charcoal bags on sale, and picked one up, remembering my bucket in the boat was empty. As my partners loaded groceries into the pick-up, I stashed that bag in the bucket under the console, and there it sat unopened — perhaps the most reassuring thing we had with us. We agreed that we would wait as long as possible to use it.

Finally, it was dark. We had done all we could do. We sat there in the roaring blizzard, tired and cold and worried, not saying much. The snow was settling in the uncovered part of the boat somewhat, since we were on the lee side of that bank. The bags of grass made a soft seat, and for the time being, we were alright. But I couldn't keep from thinking we were like three coons in a hollow tree with the hounds at the trunk, waiting for the sound of an axe. If the wind kept up, we weren't going to be as snug in the wee hours of the morning. We were going to be blown off the marsh as the water rose.

We had a thermos bottle filled with hot coffee — at least it had been hot at mid-day when I had filled it. That was seven hours before. We decided we would save it until later and share it. By 8 p.m., we had changed our minds and drank it all. Somehow, it lifted our spirits, but by then we were cold, terribly cold, despite the shelter and the heavy clothes. We walked around the boat a little, using Darrell's small flashlight to see how much snow was accumulating. It didn't seem like much for all the amount that had fallen. And it seemed as if maybe the wind was just a mite weaker with the increasing snow. From the stakes we had driven in the bank beside the boat, we could see that the water was easily a foot higher in the three hours we had been there.

Before 9 p.m. we hauled the bucket beneath the plywood and camouflage shelter, and spread a layer of charcoal over the sand. You cannot imagine the encouragement I received from that sudden burst of heat when the briquettes flamed high and began to burn. The three of us huddled over the opening of the bucket and assured each other that this would fight off the hypothermia we feared the most.

We hadn't talked a great deal about our predicament until then, like we were almost afraid to say what we were feeling. John finally remarked that he would just about trade his shotgun for something to eat, and Darrell got the idea that we could breast out one of the mallards and cook the breast over the charcoal. We used a wire to hang chunks of meat down over the glowing coals, sure that the lack of salt and seasoning would be of little consequence since we hadn't eaten in nearly 12 hours. But we were wrong. Even hungry, the meat tasted pretty bad. But we ate it, and when it was over I actually felt the meager meal had helped a little.

Nothing, though, took away the sound of the wind over the darkened marsh, and the accumulating snow which blanketed the boat. Settling out of the wind, the snow was accumulating, and though we were covered by our makeshift shelter, our boots stuck out so that we had to keep shaking the snow off them. And all three of us were having trouble keeping our feet warm.

"I don't mind losing some toes," Darrell said, in complete seriousness which was unlike him. "But I intend to live through this."

His words really shocked me, because my long-time hunting companion usually makes a joke out of everything.

"Of course we're going to live through it," I told him. "We've got everything we need to survive this cold 'til morning.

"The cold isn't our big worry," he answered. "When the water comes up another three feet and we're not sheltered by this bank behind us, we're going to be sitting in that wind, facing swells that will likely swamp this boat."

Then John spoke up.

"Not necessarily," he said. "That bay out there is deep, open water. Back in here, there's no deep water to the south, just shallow marsh and grassland. The water may come up over it, and the wind may carry us, but there won't be swells here like there are on that open bay. This boat can take some pretty rough water. We've rode some pretty good white-caps down on Bull Shoals and again on Lake of the Woods."

His words hit me hard. I had been sitting there in the cold darkness in stark fear of the inevitable trip we had to make across that big bay, knowing that if the wind didn't lay, we wouldn't make it. Suddenly I realized that our salvation would be the high water. We didn't have to go west, into the bay. We could forge due south, across the shallow marsh and reed beds to the river. Water that was normally only a few inches deep would be four or five feet deep by morning, and sand bars that couldn't be crossed during most periods would be well beneath the surface.

It might be hard to envision the impact that realization had on me that night. I stood up and turned my face into the wind, letting the snow blast my face as I held my hands high and yelled at the top of my voice. Maybe it wasn't a guaranteed thing, but we now had a chance. My boat could cross that marsh if we just showed our tail to the wind and cut through the weeds.

At first, my hunting partners thought I had gone berserk, until I explained the source of my elation. Neither of them was as sure as I was. But it did seem to be a possibility. We would be skirting the bay, and if there were no obstacles between us and the Red River two miles away, the chances were better than good. We dug the map of the marsh out of my camera box, and again using Darrell's flashlight, we huddled around the charcoal bucket to chart our course. There was one place where a high bank much like the one behind us might present a problem. I knew there were small trees along it, much like willows, and some of them pretty good size. If we had to turn around them, we'd be turning the boat broadside to the waves, and there would be danger.

I actually slept some after midnight, but it wasn't much rest. The temperature was really down there, and the wind raging. I hadn't ever known such a wind chill. But we huddled to together and kept adding charcoal and praying.

We were all religious men, but too young to be as religious as we wished we had been. I had two little girls at home, and a wonderful wife who was in church every Sunday with them. I went with them quite a bit, when the duck-hunting season was over and when the fishing wasn't real good. I knew that if I got to spend another Sunday with them in church it would be because God got us across that marsh with His hand around that boat. And I guess, as strange as it seems, just about the time the wind started hitting our little shelter pretty good, was the time I felt His presence the most. I just began to feel, somehow, that we were going to make it.

When the first light began to seep across that marsh, we had taken down the plywood and the camouflage and the bow was tied to the largest of the small shrubs. We had scooped bushels of snow out of the boat, and now the wind was sweeping off much that remained. The waves were starting to bust against the bow, and icy spray was shooting up over us, hissing against that hot bucket where the last of the charcoal burned bright.

I started the motor, and we let it warm as John prepared to cut us loose. No one had much to say. And then, in the grayness of the morning, we were floating free, the waves lifting us like a carnival ride as the motor roared into gear. At one-third throttle we edged forth across the marsh, southward. I tried to trim the motor, and keep our speed right for the waves which we had to ride. So cold I could scarcely feel my hands and feet, and with my face too stiff to talk, I felt the spray hit my coat and face and freeze. My eyes were watering, but I could see the occasional grasses sticking up here and there which the prop was cutting through.

We were doing it. We were going across that marsh with the wind and the waves and snow and we were going to have the ordeal behind us in no time at all. And then I saw the trees....

There wasn't enough light to see them far off, and they were there so quickly, a line of willow tops sticking up out of the water, some of them six or eight feet in the air. There was no gap, no opening — no chance.

And then suddenly, there was just an ever-so-small space before me. I gave the throttle a shove and the boat lunged forward, the motor roaring and the bow rising into the trees before us.

Sitting in the bottom of the boat looking backward, John didn't know what was before us. Darrell saw it coming, and ducked lower. He said later he thought it was all over just then. I felt the limbs whip me as they flew past, but I was too cold to feel them much. I did feel the prop catch something, but the steel blades cut through whatever it was, and in a second we were in open water. Minutes later we were ascending the choppy waters of Netley Creek. It was over!

I slept pretty well most of that morning, after some time in a hot shower at the cabin, and an hour or so of violent shivering that all the blankets in the world didn't seem to help. Darrell got the feeling back in his toes, though he says they hurt for a month afterward, and we ate everything we had in that cabin. By late afternoon we were headed for home.

Funny thing is, it didn't seem all that cold later in

the day when we loaded the boat and all our gear, preparing to leave Manitoba. The wind had finally subsided and there were low, broken clouds with the sun breaking through on occasion. Another place, another time, it might have been a good day to hunt ducks. But for us, it was a good day to go home.

I still go back to Manitoba every year, and most years I hunt a day or two out on Netley Marsh. But some of my hunting partners in recent years have found it to be a little strange how quick I am to pack up the decoys when the wind gets up a bit and the clouds move in low and cold. I just tell 'em I can hear the voices of old duck-hunters from years past...and I ain't as mad at the ducks as I use to be.

Chapter 7
Ghost Gobbler of
The Phantom Ridge

I don't know if I'll ever go back...there are other places to hunt wild turkey in the midwest and there are numbers of gobblers much closer to home. But I can tell you this: as long as I live to hunt, I will never forget the place my friends and I came to know as the "phantom ridge" — and a wild gobbler like none that I have hunted.

He materialized one April morning from the fog that hung heavy on a west Arkansas mountaintop. It wasn't such an unusual thing really. Every experienced turkey hunter has seen it happen; when the woods are damp and quiet and dawn seems to be dragging its feet, a gobbler materializes. He's just there, and you didn't hear him or see him or even expect him.

This one came from behind me to my left and when his movement brought my senses to full attention, he was only 25 feet away at the very most. Then he saw me.

In the few seconds it takes for everything to happen, it's surprising how much goes on in your mind. There's the immediate shift of heartbeat. The realization that this gobbler has the edge on you...and the indecision that usually gives him an even bigger edge.

But that morning something else registered in that instant of indecision. The gobbler's beard was 10 inches long, maybe 11. It wasn't unusually thick; I have several better ones on my wall in the den. But this beard was one-in-a-million. The lower two or three inches was a beige, almost white color.

As suddenly as he had appeared, he was leaving... head low, putting distance and pine trees between us in a hurry. I wanted to shoot...did I ever want to shoot. But I didn't. Even when the gobbler flew just at the edge of range. I knew I had little chance of a killing shot.

I moved up the ridge a half-mile and spent the rest of the morning waiting for the fog to lift and another gobbler to materialize.

By morning, the sun broke through, but the woods

remained quiet. At noon, I began the long walk back to camp, wondering if I would have another chance at the gobbler with the frosted beard. My spirits had lifted some...after all he wasn't going anywhere. At that same time the day before, I had been ready to give up.

Clyde and I had made a half dozen trips to the Ouachita mountains of western Arkansas. My old friend was nearing 70 years of age; he had more years of experience hunting the wild gobbler than any man I've met before or since. We usually camped in the same place and hunted the same ridges behind our camp, an area we had grown to know very well. But that year other hunters had moved in to claim our campsite, so we had been forced to a new ridge. It was a good spot to hunt, a long, fairly wide ridge where Clyde could hunt without much exertion. So we camped there — back away from the main roads, encouraged by plenty of sign even though the birds weren't gobbling much. On opening day I moved well down the ridge away from camp and the immediate area where Clyde would hunt.

I didn't hear a gobble that morning. It was chilly, so by 9 a.m. I decided maybe I'd see where this big wide ridge went to and warm up while doing it. I guess I walked two, maybe three miles, stopping to call and listen, noticing that there was indeed plenty of droppings and scratching along the ridge.

I sat down finally as the sun grew warmer and would have dozed off awhile had it not been for a crow. The black rascal was giving something what-for and it prompted a gobble strong and loud only 200 yards before me, followed by another and another.

I moved closer, confident that I had a great opportunity to bag this gobbler, even though it was nearing midday. I did something I have not very often done. I moved too close. I got within 100 yards of the gobbler, but I was moving slowly and saw him before he saw me. Unfortunately, there were four hens with that old strutting tom. Miraculously, none had seen me. Since the woodland opened a bit, I could watch them and I figured I was hidden well enough to call the whole bunch right to me.

As I called, the hens fed and the tom strutted and

As I called, the hens fed and the tom strutted and gobbled. They all moved slowly but surely the other way, finally angling down off the ridge. Then, after an hour of silence, I heard a last gobble way down below me, and I decided it was time for dinner and a nap back in camp.

Late that afternoon I went back to look over that beautiful stretch of woodland that was just torn up with the scratching of wild turkeys. I walked down off the side of the slope and found a finger coming off the ridge that was maybe 300 or 400 yards long — perpendicular to the main ridge, but jutting out above the creek valley. There were big pines along one side, and huge white oaks along another. Here, too, the leaf litter was raked up everywhere by turkeys.

The spot was so beautiful I just sat down and stayed awhile. I heard nor saw nothing that evening, but returned the following morning in the fog. That's when I first spotted that gobbler with the light-tipped beard.

As we headed homeward that spring, I told Clyde about the turkey. He said he had killed a gobbler with such a beard once, but it wasn't a ground-raker. I asked if he thought the turkey might still be there again the next season and my old friend reckoned he probably would.

"We'll get him next year then," I joked, not knowing that while that gobbler would indeed be there, Clyde would not. He died two months later of a sudden stroke.

When April finally came, I went to the Ouachita mountains without the total exhilaration felt in previous springs. I camped on that long ridge again, but this year without Clyde. With me were friends new to turkey hunting and around the campfire the evening before opening day, I gave them advice and answered their questions just as Clyde had done years before with me.

I could picture Clyde sitting there saying to me, "So, you're an expert now...?"

Many times Clyde had joked about how would-be'ers (his term for beginning turkey hunters) became authorities after they had a gobbler or two to their credit. It was my eighth year of turkey hunting and I had 22 gobblers to my credit, hunting in Missouri and Arkansas. I knew by then that any advice I gave wasn't going to help my friends as much as they'd learn by making mistakes and miscalculations and getting lucky once in awhile.

Dave Meisner and Norm Beattie had traveled from Des Moines, Iowa. for their first turkey hunt. They were much concerned about their calling and, though I assured them the calling was the least part of it, I don't think either hunter believed me.

Just before sunrise the next day, Norm called up two toms that never gobbled. He missed his shot, learning in the process that wild gobblers, which move ever so slowly as they strut before a hunter, are like streaks of lightning on two legs when they detect movement.

Dave and I headed in another direction and got a gobbler to answer our call. He was in the valley below, maybe 250 yards away, and he gobbled his head off as he came up to find us.

I situated Dave 30 yards before me on the trace of an ancient logging road. The gobbler came up that trail at a brisk pace but stopped about 60 yards from Dave. He must have sensed that something just wasn't quite right. To Dave's credit, he never moved an eyelid as the turkey circled him just out of range and walked toward me, where I dropped him at 35 yards, a 21-pound tom with a 10-inch beard.

I bragged a little on my ability to call a gobbler around another hunter and Dave labeled me a game hog, but it was great to have a turkey hanging from the camp cross-pole that afternoon.

It became a bit easier to talk like an expert; what the heck, what they didn't know wouldn't hurt nobody.

Jim Spencer, the fourth member of our group, had found the phantom ridge. I could tell by the way he spoke of it...the beauty of that ridge which dipped off into the deep valley, the abundance of sign, the stillness beneath the towering pines and hardwoods. And then there was the gobbler, a big one that came up behind him and never gobbled.

"Naw, I didn't get the son-of-a-gun," Spencer said. "He kicked leaves in my face."

I asked if he had seen a frosted beard.

"Heck no," Jim said as he dug into the ice chest for a cold soda. "I saw his eyes for a second, then the back of his feet and flying leaves..."

Evening came, and Spencer returned to camp an hour after dark shaking his head.

"I went back up there to get that turkey," he said, "and I'll be danged if I could find that finger ridge again. It's just like it disappeared. First thing I know, I got lost, and I've been trying to find camp ever since."

Jim Spencer, an outdoor writer and experienced hunter, had walked for hours finally arriving at a logging road some distance from our camp where he gained his bearings and charted a new course.

"That ridge is really a strange place," he told me. I agreed, relating my experiences the previous season. That's when we dubbed it the phantom ridge.

Jim went another direction the following day, so Dave and I made the long march along the wide ridge where the phantom ridge and the frosted-beard gobbler waited. We never found the perpendicular ridge. It was one of the most perplexing days I've ever spent turkey hunting.

We returned that evening to look again, and somehow we wound up on the phantom ridge. Dave agreed it was a fantastic spot, but there was nothing but silence. We stayed late, hoping to hear gobblers flying to roost in the valley below us, but we heard nothing. So we headed back and in the dusk and cloud cover Dave remarked that he hoped we weren't lost. I laughed and told him that in all my years in the Ozarks and Ouachitas I had never been lost.

It began to rain just after darkness set in, and I finally admitted that somehow we had indeed gotten lost. And it was no laughing matter.

The temperature had dropped to around 38 degrees and I knew that we were in for hours of steady rain. We dropped into the valley, followed a creek downstream and struck the remnants of an old logging road. We could follow it pretty well and even in the rain and darkness, I could tell a four-wheel drive vehicle had traveled it not too long before. Three hours after dusk, we tromped into a hunter's camp, cold, wet and tired. We were miles from our camp, so he gave us a ride back and we all tried to figure out why we had wound up completely opposite the direction we thought we were traveling.

Meisner went with Spencer the next morning so I took Norm Beattie with me, tromping west again along the long wide ridge beneath dripping foliage dappled with new dogwood blossoms. We stopped at the spot where I knew the phantom ridge should veer off to the right. But it wasn't there and I sure wasn't about to look for it. We were close, there were turkeys in the valley below us and there was security on the long wide ridge where camp was only a long walk toward the rising sun.

We were going to walk just a little farther but Norm said he thought he heard something. I smiled to myself, knowing that beginners often hear gobblers all night long and a week after returning from a hunt.

But to appease Norm, I gave a soft call, and immediately a gobbler answered well down the slope. Norm and I separated about 35 yards and I continued to call. The tom answered often and began moving up the slope toward us. I'll admit I thought about the gobbler with the frosted beard, but I told myself that even if the old gobbler was still there, he wouldn't gobble that much and come that readily.

But he was and he did.

I saw his head first, as before, a bright red flag jerking its way along, up the wooded hillside bobbing up and down like an apple in a hot tub. Then I saw the beard, long and slender, the last couple of inches light colored, like it had been dipped in bleach.

I was between Norm and the gobbler. If there was to be a shot, I'd have to take it. I did — at what could have been no more than 40 yards. At that distance my three-inch magnum, loaded with number fours, should have killed that turkey. But the gun or I, one, missed. The gobbler put his head down, covered 30 yards in two-and-a-half seconds and lifted into flight gliding to the valley below.

I spent that evening around the campfire wondering aloud how I could have missed. It was the first turkey I ever shot at that I didn't get. I had scared off a few — well, a whole passel, to tell the truth. I had even used two shells a one, and I suddenly remembered Clyde saying in his slow drawl, "Well, Mr. Dablemont, a hunter spends his first year or two thinking that killin' a gobbler is next to impossible, an' then he gets one or two or three. Next thing you know, he figures he's an expert 'cause it worked so well. About that time he gets too confident an' misses one or two or three. Then he starts wondering if he'll ever get another one."

I did get another one, a 17-pound jake, on the last day of our Ouachita trip that year. It was a windy morning and he gobbled like a veteran but ran to my call like a teenager at his first dance — anxious and clumsy. Jim bagged a gobbler that day, too, and we headed home with three birds between us. But I would have traded all three for one more crack at the gobbler with the frosted beard.

It was just Jim and I the following year, and he brought topographical maps that he said would help us figure out where the phantom ridge was. However, the maps showed several fingers coming off the ridge in that area, and it made it even more confusing.

"I'm gonna find that phantom ridge," Jim said, "and blaze a trail back so I can always find it again. It really gets me, to know it's there and not be able to locate it, especially when I know I have to be so close."

At daybreak the next morning, Jim and I paused on the long ridge to listen. We heard several gobblers. I went toward one, and he went toward another.

At 7 a.m., while calling one gobbler, another answered, nearly upon me. I shifted positions and waited. The tom came right in, saw me at 35 yards and dropped his head to the ground as I shot over him. When he flew, I figured he was a goner, but I missed a second time, perhaps trying too hard to put a shot only in the head. I didn't see the beard well, but I didn't think it was discolored. I kicked a stump or two and cussed my rotten luck.

Right there on that ridge I had missed two turkeys in two seasons after eight years of hunting. And if I had known what lay ahead, I would have returned to camp. However, an hour later I heard another gobbler some distance away down in the valley where the first bird had flown. So I went down in the valley where the first bird had flown. So I went after it. I called to the gobbler from two locations and he answered me fairly well but didn't move much. Unfamiliar with the lay of that creek valley, I decided that there was some obstacle between us. There was — a small fork in the creek. Once I got across it, the gobbler was close enough to shake hands with. I saw him stick his head up over a small draw, and then stand there looking at me. It would have to be a quick shot. I tried it but the gobbler was much faster than I was and I didn't catch another glimpse of him until he was well out of range.

As I sat in camp and felt sorry for myself that afternoon, bad weather moved in and by evening a storm was upon us.

Jim and I traded sad stories as rain and wind pelted our tent. It continued the next morning so I stayed in camp. Jim went out and got wet, only to return and report that the gobblers had been silent. Throughout that day the wind was so bad there was little chance to hear or be heard. But during the night the sky cleared and the woods grew quiet. The sun would rise to a cloudless sky and the pines would stand still and silent. The stage was set for a final meeting with the ghost gobbler of phantom ridge.

Somehow I staggered onto the narrow, sloping saddle that led to the ridge. In the first light of day, I admired its beauty again. Along the west side, where the pines were largest, there was something of a bluff that provided an overview of the valley below. It wasn't exactly a bluff, but it was steep, too steep to walk down. I sat down and called once. A gobbler answered on the other side of the ridge which sloped gently into a hardwood forest. The gobbler sounded quite a ways down the ridge, so I moved closer.

Slowly moving towards the gobbler, I caught a glimpse of him, maybe 100 yards ahead. Dropping beside a big white oak, I called again, and the gobbler headed toward me with two hens behind him. He stopped at 80 yards and began to strut, gobbling occasionally as he moved in small compact circles. He was a big, beautiful gobbler, but that wasn't what made my hands shake. It was the beard — nearly a foot long it seemed — and the lower tip off-colored, appearing nearly white. It just had to be that same gobbler from the previous two years.

As he strutted, circled and gobbled, one of the hens came to me on a run. She stopped only 10 or 15 yards away, and though I hugged the white oak as still as a statue, she knew there was danger. Perking softly, she returned to the gobbler, then both hens headed for the valley. The old tom strutted and gobbled awhile longer, as I called. But he finally followed the hens. For an hour or so, he gobbled regularly in the valley below. By mid-morning he was quiet, but I hadn't given up. The valley was deep and the ridge on the other side was a rough climb, but I decided I would have a better chance there.

Often hens will leave a gobbler after early morning mating activity. If that happened, I would still have a chance. So I climbed to the opposite ridge, found a good sunny spot and lay down to take a short nap. About 10 a.m. the old gobbler confirmed my suspicions that he'd remained in the valley by waking me with a gobble. He ignored my calling for 15 minutes, then he gobbled again. By 11 a.m. he was gobbling consistently but he wasn't heading my way. He was working, ever so slowly, back up the steep side of the phantom ridge toward his early morning strutting ground. I'd have to try to beat him back there.

It took me 20 minutes to cross the big hollow, circling wide around the gobbler, hurrying over big rocks and fallen trees, sometimes having to move up the steep incline on all fours. But I beat him. And I set up in a small thicket very close to the place he had frequented at dawn. I listened as the big tom gobbled down the hill only a hundred yards or so. Breathing heavily, I hoped I had enough time to regain my strength.

I called only once and the gobbler quickly answered, 30 yards closer. I knew it was only a matter of time. I finally saw him, 50 yards away coming up the slope at a steady pace. There it was — the long, light-tipped beard flopping back and forth as he walked. My heart switched into overdrive and I squeezed my shotgun with the anticipation of success. He was at 45 yards, I needed only a few more steps. Beneath my breath, I begged him to keep coming.

At 40 yards he stopped, head high, watching and waiting. He puffed up, gobbled again, then waited and watched. Finally, he stepped up on an old log, determined to stay as the morning dragged on.

I could get him, I knew! He stayed there huffing up into strutting posture, then standing straight with head high. I prayed that he'd jump off that log and move forward, because a small tree between us protected his head much of the time.

After 20 minutes, I began to think I should take the quick shot. With a small move to my right with the shotgun, I could avoid the sapling. My eyes were watering, and my vision, so concentrated on one object for so long, was becoming hazy.

A blue jay shrieked nearby. The gobbler's head came up and my shotgun was at my shoulder in the blink of an eyelash. I leaned to the right and the woods echoed with the blast.

I came to my feet a fraction of a second after the number four shot hit home, aware that I had lost the feeling in my right leg, aware that the gobbler was down, hit hard. In his death throes, the big bird gained his feet and for just a minute, I thought he would go back down. His wings drooped and it was plain he would not fly away.

Flopping and falling, he headed up behind me, toward the west side of the ridge and the bluff. I knew that if he'd head down the hill where he came from, I'd intercept the gobbler. But if he gained the bluff, I'd have no chance. Hurriedly, I squeezed off a second shot but his head was down and I either missed or the body protected the head and neck of the tom. With one shot left, I ran after the gobbler as hard as I could run, aware that it was a dangerous thing to do, but knowing full well I had to gain ground before the gobbler reached that high ground.

He seemed to gain strength as I lost mine. When I last saw him, he was 50 yards away and the bluff was before him.

With all my strength expended, I gasped for air and on my hands and knees looked over the steep rock hillside where the gobbler had disappeared.

the 100 yard uphill sprint that had taken everything I had. But eventually I skirted the bluff and searched futilely in the steep rocky ground below. I had called him in, I had outsmarted him, I had killed him. I conceded defeat.

I knew that night, as I sat at the campfire's edge listening to the owls and the coyotes deep in the darkened forest, that the gobbler with the frosted beard was no more. And on this day, once again and for the last time, the old gobbler had beaten me. He was the victor after all.

The next year Jim Spencer and I returned to the Ouachita Mountains to find a newly constructed Forest Service road along the mountain we had hunted for so long. Wide enough for two big semi's, the road is a super structure that cost millions in taxpayer dollars. The massive clear-cut underway made the area unrecognizable. The beautiful forested mountain is now an ugly scar, a desert of stumps and slash. And, like the gobbler with the frosted beard, the phantom ridge is no more.

Maybe, someday, the forces of nature will prevail and trees will grow again where the gravel road winds. Maybe there'll be wind in majestic pines along the phantom ridge when today's fresh cut stumps have long decayed. And, maybe there'll be a wise old gobbler and his harem and the challenge of another spring hunt.

Chapter 8
Catfish That Size
Don't Ever Die

With the clouds moving in low and thick, daylight was fading faster than usual, and dusk made the yawning mouth of the big cave a welcome sight. Occasionally a flash of lightning interrupted the darkness and peals of thunder followed.

Grandpa was right again, a storm was on its way. He trudged up the path in front of me, toward the cave where we had our camp made. Stormy June nights were great for trotlining, but they weren't much for open camping.

If the lightning and rain could be weathered on a gravel bar, the wind couldn't, so Grandpa usually chose a protective cave for overnight shelter. There were lots of caves along the Piney and so there was a nearby shelter for most of the quiet, deep eddies where big flathead catfish lurked.

The Henry Hayes eddy was maybe the best trotlining hole of all, so grandpa claimed. We floated down from the Sand Shoals crossing early in the afternoon with food, bedding, and trotlines. We set up camp in the cave up on the wooded hillside at the head of the eddy, then set a pair of lines beneath the big bluff downstream a ways. After the lines were set, we paddled on down seining the shoals for bait. Thirty minutes before dusk, with lines baited, we still had several dozen big doughgut minnows and small longear sunfish, and there were even a few horny head chubs about six or seven inches long, which grandpa claimed was a favorite food of big cat.

I was wet to my armpits, tired and hungry as we entered the cave. I changed into dry clothes as Grandpa poured water in carbide lamps and lit the spout of gas that poured forth, filling the cave with a dim glow that left flick-

---

(Photo left:) My Grandfather's biggest flathead catfish—about 65 pounds — taken on the night I was born.

ering shadows on the rock walls.

With wood we had gathered earlier, he built an open fire that started small and grew slowly. An old blackened iron grill rested on rocks which lay to either side of the flame. I filled a coffee pot from the stream at the back of the cave while Grandpa fried potatoes and fish for supper in a big iron skillet.

There was another flash of lightning and a sudden roar of thunder overhead. Outside, you could hear big drops, splattering against the oak leaves as the rain began suddenly, then stopped again as abruptly as it had begun.

"It's a-tryin' mighty hard t'come a frog-stranglin' flood tonight," Grandpa said over the sizzle of hot grease. "Sure as thunder, we'll wind up losin' them lines after workin' so hard to get 'em set an' baited proper. 'Course, you got to have a storm to get the big 'uns, so maybe I oughten t' complain."

"Maybe we can get the lines run once or twice before the river comes up," I said, "like we did that night up at the Sweet 'Tater eddy."

My grandfather and I had been trotlining since early April that year. He was bent on teaching a 13-year-old boy the things he knew best, the things that had brought him a local reputation as a riverman.

We had taken a pair of big flathead, 18 and 23 pounds at the Sweet Potato eddy in May, just before a downpour that brought the river up four feet and washed our lines away.

Trotlining, as I was learning, was hard work. A line had to be set just right to produce fish. Grandpa would usually angle his line across the river from a root or sapling on one side, tight across the surface to the opposite bank. Then he would go back and add big number six-ought hooks on 15 inch stagings, about three-feet apart. Between every four hooks he would place a rock about the size of a fist. The nylon line would stretch, and the weights would carry it down to lay across the bottom, where the big catfish lurked. Handling the heavy line not only chapped and cracked the hands, it was very dangerous.

You could easily become hooked or entangled and

carried to the bottom by the weighted line.

Grandpa had always made a living on the river, by trapping, guiding, building john-boats and selling fish. Trotlines produced big catfish that brought good prices in local towns, so he became good at setting them. In fact, he became the best. Now, though laws forbade the sale of fish, Grandpa could not give it up. It was in his blood, like the rest of the river.

We were finishing supper when the rain finally began, and the wind picked up. Amidst the rumble of thunder, you could hear the wind whipping through the valley, and see the tree limbs bending in the storm when sudden flashes made it bright as day outside.

Peering out into the storm, grandpa spoke, "Reckon that'll make that big feller down there beneath that bluff come out on the prowl tonight."

"It's hard to believe there's catfish that size in the Piney," I said, carefully picking the bones from a last piece of fish.

"Well there is," he answered. "Wouldn't of believed no such story, 'lessen I hadn't seen 'im myself two year ago. I was standin' up on that bluff, huntin' a turtle to shoot, when this big log commences to move out in shaller water. Only it weren't no log; it was a catfish the likes of somethin' you'd never believe.

"He moved to shaller water to spawn, then moved back. I been tryin' now for two years to get him on a trotline. Reckon I may never."

"How much do you figger he'd weigh now?" I asked.

"Dunno," Grandpa answered, "'Spect he was 50, maybe 60 poun's then. Now...who knows, maybe close to 70 or 80 poun's"

"Maybe he died over the winter," I suggested.

Grandpa snorted, "Catfish that size don't never die — 'til somebody catches 'em." He stopped and chuckled to himself, remembering an incident from the past.

"I heer'd ol' Lumas Moore seen him las' summer an liked to kilt hisself tryin' to shoot 'im. Dived under with a .22 rifle like a derned fool and tried to shoot that big cat.

Lucky he had a friend to drag 'im out. The percussion knocked ol' Lumas out an' busted a eardrum.

"Lumas went an' tol' ever'body 'bout that catfish an' nobody believed him. Figgered him to be drunk or somethin'."

Grandpa laughed again, and waited for a burst of thunder to subside before continuing. "Me, I kept shut about that big feller. Nobody's gonna believe it. 'Sides that, I wanta ketch 'im myself."

Near exhaustion, I lay down on a bed of heavy, musty-smelling canvas tarpaulin and quilts, listening to Grandpa expound on the biggest catfish in the Big Piney.

Over his voice came intermediate claps of thunder and the steady patter of rain filtering through the trees outside.

I drifted off to sleep, secure despite the storm.

Grandpa awakened me around midnight. The rain had stopped though lightning still flashed occasionally, and thunder, while distant, could still be heard.

Rain still dripped steadily from the leaves above to patter among the under-story. We had a cup of coffee as I tried to shake off the sleep.

"Don't know if its quit fer the night, or just slackin' up a bit so's we can run our lines," Grandpa said as he slurped coffee strong enough to kill sprouts. "But it'll take us awhile to rebait the line so you'd best put on a slicker."

Moments later, with carbide headlamps lighting the path, I moved awkwardly toward the awaiting john-boat in an oversized army poncho.

Though the rain had stopped, dripping foliage made the raincoat necessary.

I waited on the bank as my grandfather used a boat paddle to splash an inch or so of water from one end of the boat. Then we moved downstream. The storm had silenced the river, even the whippoorwills. Only occasional thunder interrupted the slurp of the boat paddle entering and leaving the water as we moved along.

The water had grown slightly murky, but it seemed no higher than it had been at dusk. Grandpa found our first line and lifted it with his boat paddle for me to take.

As I moved along it, inspecting hooks that for the most part still held live healthy bait, I felt the sharp tug of a catfish out toward the middle.

I caught a glimpse of a brown body rolling across the surface and as Grandpa offered advice, I moved close. It was no monstrous flathead but a good one for the table. He weighed perhaps eight or nine pounds and, after a brief lunge or two, he came up just right. As I had been taught, I held the line firmly in one hand, and with the other, grasped the catfish tightly by the lower jaw.

He relaxed as I put pressure on the jaw and hauled him over the side. I admired him as Grandpa prepared to run the second line, which slid down into deep water and ran within six feet of a magnificent submerged boulder that probably at one time had been a part of the bluff.

My grandfather had scarcely picked up the line when he whistled beneath his breath. "Got a fair one out toward that rock!" he exclaimed, looking backwards as he moved along the line and pulled us closer to the fish. I caught a glimpse of a broad tail which splashed water into the boat as we drew up alongside.

The trotline jumped in Grandpa's hands as the three-foot-long flathead lurched against it. I watched as he let the fish go awhile, then quickly, deftly, moved his four fingers beneath the lower jaw, his thumb inside the gaping mouth. An iron grasp stilled the big cat, and moments later he lay in the boat, whipping his tail and flaring those big gills in the dim light.

"What'll he go?" I asked.

"Twenty-five, give or take two pounds," Grandpa answered, preparing to rebait the now-limp trotlines. "Well, he may be that big one's grandson, but he ain't no closer than that to the catfish that's king of this here eddy."

It started to rain again, lightly, so we hurried through the rebaiting. Near the submerged rock, Grandpa hooked the big horny-head chubs through the lips.

"Nothin'll come closer to catchin' him than one of these chubs," he exclaimed. "One of these days he'll latch onto one an' I'll have me a catfish bigger'n you are."

It was raining hard again when I slipped beneath the

quilts for the second time, and quickly dozed off, thinking of the king of the flathead catfish that lay beneath that big bluff.

Intermittently through the night, I awakened to flashes of lightning and loud thunder. The rain was slow and steady, and I figured we'd again have a rising river to cope with.

At daybreak, the storm was gone. A few clouds lingered, but not enough to keep the sun from erupting over the eastern horizon, sending its rays into the mouth of the cave.

Had it not been for the storm, we might have run and rebaited our lines again before sunrise. If he was several years younger, Grandpa would have done it anyway, but he wouldn't fish as hard with me along. Maybe later, as I grew older.

The Piney looked like it was up an inch or so, and a milky green color now. Our two catfish lay in the boat in a half-inch of water, still lively, but too big and heavy to do much more than flop back and forth.

Our first line was limp, so we moved on to the second. When Grandpa picked it up, it was tight and instead of running straight across, it angled in beneath the big rock, hopelessly entangled. He pulled against it with all his strength, maneuvering and twisting the line to get it loose. After a few minutes, the hook pulled free and the line came to the top.

"Six feet away from that rock, an' tight as I could get it, but that dern fish was strong enough to get the line hung up somewheres, then pull against it solid. That's just what this feller done."

He continued to look at the hook, shaking his head. "I'll know better next time. He's just too big for a line 'lessen you set it a long ways from this rock. We'll come back this summer a time or two and get this ol' catfish again."

Just after noon, we paddled up the river, with our trotlines and camping gear loaded in the boat with our catfish. Dad would soon be meeting us at the Sand Shoals crossing in the pickup, and I couldn't wait to show him the catfish we had taken. To me, a 20-pound catfish was a monster. I couldn't imagine one four times his size, though I knew Grandpa had caught 50 to 70 pound catfish out of the Gasconade and Osage rivers.

I looked back at the Henry Hayes bluff still showing above the sycamores around the bend.

"It's a shame you couldn't have got that big one," I said. My grandfather, laboring against the current, just snorted.

"A good foxhound don't wanta ketch the fox, just chase 'im," he said. "I'd a-soon try to ketch that big devil, 10 times, than ketch him once. When I get him, I got nothin' to look forward to."

Since that day, I've learned to enjoy each fishing trip a little more, knowing the responsibility of a good foxhound. I've come to find that the true sportsman, whether a hunter, or fisherman, is not so concerned with catching as he is with chasing. When it's the other way around, someone is missing something.

Grandpa is gone now, but the big catfish up at the Henry Hayes eddy, king of the flathead catfish in the Piney, is still there. As far as I'm concerned he always will be... because "catfish that size never die 'til somebody catches 'em."

Chapter 9
Silent Jack and
The Master

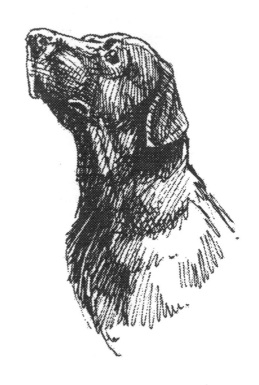

T he young man in the worn and yellowing 1927 newspaper clipping didn't look much like the aging riverman that sat before me telling of the Ozarks he had known in his youth.

But somehow, in the glow of the kerosene lantern which lit the little four-room cabin on Brushy Creek, those days did not seem so far back at all.

My grandfather was one of the last of a dying breed, a man who had lived with the land, not from it. He was as much a part of the Ozarks as the white bluffs and sycamores that watched over the Big Piney. The years and the elements that had carved the shape of those rock bluffs had put the deep lines in his face and scars on his leathery hands, and turned a heavy head of hair to white. The river had molded him to one of its own kind and he became part of its history.

His home was the home of a riverman. Grandpa had built it, and he had built the furniture in it, from table and bed to the rocking chair in which he now sat, recalling the years of his youth.

The walls, bathed in the faint, flickering light, were adorned with the tools of a riverman. Steel traps hung from nails on one wall, well-oiled, yet rust-colored from years of use. Hip boots hung in a corner; beneath them were handmade trot-line spools, with sharp hooks wrapped in brown paper, strings attached. His guns hung from wooden pegs, with hand made cleaning rods with them. His ax leaned against the wall behind the wood stove which gave the cabin a faint smell of woodsmoke, to blend with the oil and kerosene odor. This, along with the bucket of water and dipper, told the visitor that this home was without modern conveniences.

It was quiet and secluded there, you could hear the whisper of running water from the creek and a fox barking from the other side of the stream amongst the heavy timber.

In this stillness, I could almost hear the bell that hung from Silent Jack's throat on those coon hunts long ago.

Silent Jack, Grandpa called him, because he never

barked on the trail. He was there, too, in that 1927 newspaper clipping from the *St. Louis Globe Democrat*, and in the faded picture he didn't look like much of a dog.

Of mixed breed, he had the muzzle of a hound, with the strong muscular body of a hunting dog. But his ears were shorter, and his fur a little longer and heavier, coloring ranging from gray and brown to black.

Jack was more than a coon dog to Grandpa, he was a companion. He was with him on those long, lonely trapping excursions, gone for days at a time, running the length of the Big Piney in the face of the Ozarks winter, sleeping beneath bluffs and in caves along the stream.

Running a river trapline was work.

"I'd float down early, settin' my traps as I went," Grandpa said, "then camp at the end of the line. Next mornin' we'd run the ol' boat back up river three, four or five miles; however fer it was to the commencin' of my traps."

Sometimes he'd run the same line for several days, then move on downstream. If the catch was poor, he might pick up all his traps and move downriver to new territory.

His trapline was a river trapline, each trap set in a manner known as a "drown-set," which immediately drowned the mink, beaver or muskrat caught. Running traplines took a good part of the morning, and skinning and drying pelts took the remainder of it. The early part of the afternoon was then spent moving on downstream resetting the traps. By late afternoon, Grandpa would stop, make camp, eat and sleep. Before midnight, he would awaken, and he and Jack would hunt coons until sometime in the morning on the heavily timbered watershed.

Silent Jack was known as a silent trailer, and very efficient, perhaps more so than baying hounds because of his ability to trail closer and tree sooner.

Grandpa followed Jack by listening for the turkey bell attached to his collar.

"He was the grittiest coon-dog I ever owned," he told me that night, "but all the coon hunters in the country with their pure-bred hounds just laughed at ol' Jack."

"He didn't have no ribbons, but he done his job, an' he was good enough to do what them other hounds couldn't do— tree the smartest and biggest danged coon that ever lived in these parts...the one we all called the Master."

With a sigh, Grandpa leaned back in his rocker and ran a gnarled hand through snow white hair, turning back the yellow pages of time.

In the little cabin overlooking Brushy Creek, my mind went back with him nearly 50 years to that December night when Silent Jack and the Master met beneath that big white bluff overlooking the Cathcart eddy.

Silent Jack with one of the Dablemont youngsters and a raccoon in the 1930s. Note the small bell around the dog's neck.

It was a week after the big fight. Fen Marlow's two fine black-and-tan hounds were dead, and among the rivermen and farm families along the Big Piney, the big coon known as the Master had achieved notoriety.

85

The two hounds had crossed the trail of the coon, and had him a good mile from the bluff on the other side of the river. In that bluff, he had always found refuge in caves and holes where men and dogs could not follow.

The old coon had somehow learned not to seek safety in the branches of trees. The Cathcart bluff, pocketed with ledges and deep caves had become a home and an penetrable fortress against all enemies.

But finally he had been surprised, too far away from the river, raiding a small cornfield which provided better and easier meals than the quest for mussels and frogs along the river.

It was a down-hill flight to the river, but the hounds were good ones, quickly set on the hot trail and gaining ground. There was no time for the elusive stunts the Master had used so often to lose his pursuers. No time for fence-walking or backtracking, or jumping from one tree to another. He made a straight dash to the river and the protective bluff, hard pressed by the baying hounds.

The old coon made it to the river and the hounds caught him there. Instinct told him that he would lose the battle on solid footing, so he plunged into the deep water where he would have the decided advantage. In mid-stream he waited for the hounds, which were only a few feet behind him now.

Fen Marlowe and his sons had heard the chase commence and they began following at a leisurely pace expecting the coon to tree quickly in such a heated and frenzied chase.

But as the hounds grew closer to the river, they realized the sudden danger and broke into a run for the stream.

When they reached the bank the fight was over. One of Marlow's sons thought he glimpsed the hulking form of the victor leaving the water across the river in the beam of the carbide lamp.

But Fen Marlow's prize hounds did not follow. They were floating lifelessly in the river, drowned by an opponent half their size. By the size of the track in the mud of the river bank, there was little doubt that this was the biggest coon the Big Piney had seen in many a year. Saddened

Saddened deeply by the loss of his hounds, the hunter warned others to stay away from the big coon and his stomping grounds around the Cathcart eddy. As the story of the fight circulated, the old coon gained his name. The men who sat around the stove at Venable's store on those cold winter evenings spoke of him often. Some claimed their hounds had held his trail, but when it could be followed at all, it always led to the caves in the Cathcart bluff, high above the ground.

It was December when my Grandfather, only 24 at the time, made camp just upriver from the Cathcart hole. Behind him on the river lay four miles of trapline. He was a loner, setting and running his traplines from his john-boat with only his dog, Jack, as a companion. By mid afternoon that day he prepared his furs to dry. Mink and muskrat skinned easily and were stretched flesh-side out over a strong fork, cut from a limb along the stream. Beaver were much harder to skin. The pelts had to be cut from the carcass inch-by-inch, then stretched and laced circularly on a hoop formed by a bent sapling.

Grandpa's month's catch would be taken to St. Louis soon by train, and he would take up his trapline for the Christmas season. It had been a good year so far. Fur prices were good, and a trapper who was willing to brave the ice and cold of the river found furbearers plentiful.

On that December day, the young man finished a modest meal in the early afternoon, then prepared to sleep away the remaining hours of light. That night, for the fifth time in the past month, he and Jack would go out in search of one particular quarry, the coon that had won the name of the Master, and the respect of the Big Piney community.

Against the rock face of a shallow cave he prepared his bed between the rock and the fire where the heat would be held and reflected best. Every hour or two, he would replenish the fire and the reflected heat would allow him to sleep comfortably despite the winter chill. Through the afternoon, the temperature would remain pleasant, but by dark the chill would make the warm rock-face the best place to sleep.

It was late in the evening when the trapper awakened for the last time. Rising and shaking the sleep from his eyes, he replenished the fire, and soon had a flame surging from a bed of dying coals.

Jack moved away from the fire and lay down again as if knowing a long night lay ahead and there was little time left to rest.

As the young man set a pot of coffee beside the fire, he spoke to his dog: "'Bout time to eat a bit, Jack. The coons'll be movin' tonight... it's a good one for it, not too cold, good and dark. I swear, if this weather holds we'll take more fur this year than I ever knowed to be took. Don't know though, I seen mild Decembers before, and right behind 'em a rip-snortin' winter with snow an' ice an' cold winds right through January an' up to March."

Two hours before midnight, dog and hunter left the camp.

He carried a single-shot, falling-block Stevens rifle, almost a new one. It had cost him two-and-a-half dollars, and had taken nearly two months to arrive. This was a gun to be proud of, and he meant to take care of it. Ammunition was a luxury, so he didn't fire the rifle unless it was absolutely necessary. And when he fired it, he made sure of his shot. With him, he carried a string with a small strip of cloth on one end and a small ball of lead on the other. Drawing the cloth through the barrel on the string every five or six shots served to keep lead and burned powder out of the riflings of the bore and protect the gun.

With him, too, he carried an ax. When Jack treed, he often cut the tree down, and let the dog kill the coon. If it was too big to cut, he would climb it, and force the coon to jump. Decades later, it would seem an inhumane way of hunting, but in that day it was looked upon differently. Timber was plentiful and coons were thick, while ammunition was precious. It was difficult also to draw a bead on any target in the subdued light of the carbide miner's lamp which he wore on his head.

Silent Jack ranged before him, not really acting like a coon dog. The turkey bell attached to his collar was the only means of keeping up with him once he found a trail, for he seldom barked, but until he discovered a fresh trail, he didn't venture far afield from the hunter.

Coon hides were worth four to five dollars to the young Ozarkian, and that made Jack, who found and treed the coons, worth considerably more to him than anything that anyone in those parts had to offer.

Fen Marlowe, with the finest hounds in the country had ridiculed Jack and the idea of a silent trailer. Marlowe was a farmer, and one of the area's most successful ones. He had as many as 50 hogs on free-range. Each year, when hogs were rounded up for shipping and butchering, Fen Marlowe's undercropped ear brand was sure to show up more often than any other. He had money, and could afford well-bred dogs. He had always scorned the young trapper who lived in caves part of the winter and made his living from the furs he sold. Marlowe had made Silent Jack a standing joke around the local settlements. But now, Fen Marlowe's dogs were dead, and the riverman meant to show folks that Silent Jack could do what those well-bred hounds had not, find and tree the big coon which dwelled in the Cathcart eddy bluffs, the one known as the Master. Tonight would be the fifth attempt at accomplishing the feat. Four times before, Jack had been unable to find the trail of the big coon, sometimes sidetracked by trails of others.

Together, the dog and hunter continued downriver, with the soft clang of the turkey bell the only sound above the water's flow. Finally the big Cathcart bluff loomed across the river. They crossed a small creek which was nearly dry. Up this creek was the cornfield that was so popular with raccoons.

It was at this tributary that Jack picked up his first trail. Suddenly excited, he left the hunter and, nose to the ground, headed swiftly up the creek bed away from the river. At that time, the Master was at the cornfield, stripping a corncob and, ever alert, remaining unaware of the dog rapidly piecing together his trail.

The sound of bells was not strange to the raccoon. Free-ranging cattle, goats and turkeys at that time wore bells in order to make them easier to find. But the sound the Master heard that night was surely a hint of something out of place. Instead of the occasional clank of metal around the neck of a feeding goat, this was a constant sound reflecting hurried movements.

But likely, the raccoon was not too alarmed. The baying which he associated with dogs was not heard, just the sound of the approaching bell.

As the clanking grew louder, the coon took flight, merely from caution, not fear; he didn't expect the sound to follow him. Approximately 100 yards from the cornfield, the old raccoon became aware that the strange bell was pursuing him. And once again, through a different set of circumstances, the Master knew that his pursuer was much too close, and the safety of the Cathcart bluff much too far away. Experience told him that, if caught, his best chance was at the river, so again his course was direct and swift.

Grandpa Dablemont with his dog Jack and a 1927 cache of furs.

At this point, the trail became easier for Jack to follow. It was hot and straight, so he gained ground.

The young hunter had not followed his dog, anticipating the chase to return toward the river, and now he was positioned upstream about 75 yards from the Master's crossing point at the lower end of the eddy.

When the coon reached that point, he headed upstream about 15 yards to the steepest bank, where the water was deep, and plunged in. Now he was in no hurry. If he was to be caught, the fight would be to his advantage in the water. But his foe, which had drawn so close in the chase across the bottom, didn't follow. He crossed downstream, on a shoal where the water was shallow, and reached the opposite bank at the same time his quarry climbed from the water.

The Cathcart bluff loomed upriver only 30 or 40 yards, and the Master headed for it. Halfway, Silent Jack caught him, and on solid footing, the ensuing fight was evenly matched.

Across the river, the riverman heard the fight, and he splashed through the shallow water of the nearest shoal, icy water wetting him to the thighs.

Jack was a fighter, and equal to any coon hound, but if this was the Master, he was up against a coon capable of whipping any good hound.

Before he could reach them, the fight had ended. But the sound of the turkey bell could still be heard. Somehow, the coon had broke free and chose to take to the protection of the branches.

When the hunter reached the tree, he found Jack, bloody with a torn ear and in the upper branches of the big sycamore he caught his first glimpse of the Master. The big boar coon had not given up. He was pacing the long limb, looking toward the rock bluff nearly 12 feet beyond. He knew he had to jump for it, and the young man below knew what he had in mind.

He raised his rifle, but then lowered it. A still target would have been hard to hit, much less this moving one.

This was the coon that had whipped Fen Marlowe's hounds, though outnumbered. This was the Master, bigger than any he'd seen before on the Piney, smart enough to become that old and big despite the hunters who had tried to take him. His pelt would be worth more than any he had ever taken, and the satisfaction gained from showing the local people Jack's true ability would be great indeed.

He knew the Master was preparing to jump for the safety of the bluff, and that there was no chance of Jack getting him now unless he failed to make the jump.

Still he could not shoot. This old coon was a lot like him, a loner, a river dweller, not asking much out of life, just freedom and solitude. He was worth more than a chance shot in the dark which could not even insure a quick death. If he could make that jump, he deserved to live, if he didn't...

Slowly the hunter lowered the rifle, and watched as the Master jumped for the bluff ledge. The old coon gave it every ounce of energy he had. As he left the limb, it swayed in the darkness, and a shadow plunged through the air barely reaching the bluff and avoiding the 20 foot fall. He clung precariously to a slight ledge for a moment, then gained his balance and was gone.

Beneath the bluff, the young man restrained his dog. They crossed the Piney and he quickly built a fire to dry his wet and cold feet. In the flicker of the flame, Jack continued to look toward the big bluff. Removing his wet boots to allow them to dry over the fire, the hunter consoled him.

"Aw, don't take it so hard, Jack, it don't matter. They's plenty of other coons. You don't have to prove nothin' to nobody, you're as good a coon hound as they is anywheres. I know that, an' you know it." He paused a moment and gazed toward the white bluff looming across the river.

"An I reckon that ol' coon laid up in that bluff yonder knows, too."

Chapter 10
Tommy's Brother

M y mother's father sold his farm when I was 14-years old and he and my grandmother moved to town. He said he was too old to milk and feed chickens and tend a garden. I didn't know then how much I'd miss that 140 acres. The creek and the pond full of bullfrogs and bluegill provided my cousins and me hours of boyhood fun, days that I will recall with fond memories all of my life.

In those days there were fence-rows full of rabbits and quail, and wood lots where fox-squirrels worked over acorns and hickories. Occasionally you saw a deer, maybe a track at the pond or in a muddy tractor rut coming from the creek. Of course, there were no wild turkey around. But heck, quail, rabbits, squirrels and an occasional deer track were enough. That farm seemed a wilderness to my cousins and me.

Then suddenly it was gone, and it would be twenty years before I saw those familiar spots again.

I guess several owners followed my grandpa, but eventually J. D. Stillwater bought the property. He owned much of the land from the small town where I grew up eastward to my grandfather's place which was about five or six miles out of town. J. D. was easily the richest man in the county, and a lot of folks hated him because of it. But he had always treated me especially nice, maybe because he liked my grandfather.

One year, Stillwater told me I was welcome to go see the old place anytime.

"Lots of deer and turkey in there now," he said, "you're welcome to hunt it if you'd like."

In September, I took my wife and kids back into the far reaches of the old farm, though they didn't seem as far as they once did. The old farmhouse burned several years ago. There's nothing there now but a foundation, and weeds growing where a lawn had been. I showed my daughters the old well and where the barn had been. The orchard was in bad shape, but there were still some apples on a few trees and we ate around the worm holes, just like I did as a kid.

Stillwater ran cattle over most of his land and logged some of it. But I had to admit, he didn't overgraze, and he didn't wipe out the timber for a quick buck. The old farm looked good. One of the ponds had dried up and was filled in, but the big one down by the creek had been rebuilt. The creek was clear and cold, and the swimming hole still there. I remember thinking as a boy that it was 10 feet deep and a hundred feet across. It's funny how much smaller a swimming hole gets when you aren't afraid of the water any more.

The sycamore tree on the creek was huge. Twenty years ago it was a third that size. Tommy Moreland and I used to swing into the creek on an overhanging limb.

There was a great deal of sadness in that memory. Tommy, my boyhood friend, had been killed in Viet Nam in 1968. It was often that way back then — the top half of the class went to college, the lower half went into the service. For some reason, it was always the poorer kids who wound up in the bottom half of the class. I was right in the middle — and luckier than some.

The Morelands still lived on their small place behind my grandfather's old farm. The old man didn't work; he had long since given up. They lived mostly on what they raised and welfare.

When Tommy and I were young, he was a proud man, young and hard working. I remember my grandfather saying he was a good man, he liked him. Then Tommy was killed and Mr. Moreland turned bitter and hard. There were six other children in the family, some of them still fairly young and living at home.

Stillwater claimed that the biggest threat to turkey and deer on my grandfather's old place was the Moreland kid.

"If you ever see him on that land," he told me, "tell him to get the heck off. I know dern well I've lost more than one calf to those people, let alone the deer and turkey they poach."

Those words stung a bit. Stillwater had so much and

those people had so little. I remembered them from the days when Tommy and I were boys and I couldn't accept them as thieves.

I didn't know, during that September visit with my kids that I'd be back in November hunting the old farm, but it worked out that way. Stillwater said I'd have the place to myself, and there were some big bucks back across the creek in the persimmon groves and thickets around the big pond.

I took his word for it. It isn't a good idea to hunt deer on the spur of the moment, but I just didn't have time to do any pre-season scouting. The afternoon before opening day I carried a Baker climbing tree-stand back to the pond and found a nice straight red oak that overlooked the creek and the persimmon grove that had once been a pasture.

On opening day I sat in my tree-stand waiting for the sunrise, my thoughts 20 years away, centered on sunrise in the old farmhouse, a crackling wood stove, and breakfast of gravy, biscuits and sausage before heading for the barn with my grandparents to "do the chores."

Thirty minutes after first light, the wind picked up a bit and it began to get chilly. I heard a shot in the distance and within seconds a shotgun report that sounded as if it were less than 100 yards to my right. As the roar of the gun echoed across the valley, a big buck stumbled through the fringe of oak trees and into the open, obviously hit hard. He staggered toward the creek and went down. I waited and watched, my eyes fixed on what was obviously a dandy buck, maybe eight or 10 points. In a few moments a young boy appeared, he came through the oaks following the blood trail. When he spied the downed buck, I figured he'd let out a real war-hoop, but he didn't. Instead, he admired the buck for a moment, then bent over and began to gut it.

He was so involved in his work, he didn't hear me walk up behind him. He was dressed in an old army jacket that was too big for him and wore tennis shoes that were wet with dew. His shotgun was an old 12-gauge single-shot with a broken forearm that had been taped.

"That's a nice buck you got there, son," I said.

Surprised, he wheeled and stared at me with eyes

the size of saucers, sheer terror on his face. My heart jumped as I looked into the face of my boyhood friend. Then I realized this was surely his little brother.

The boy stood and dropped the knife, looking at the ground. "I guess you got me dead-handed, Mister," he said.

"You mean red-handed." I couldn't help but smile. "What's your name?"

"Clint Moreland," the boy said. "You one of Stillwater's men?" I shook my head. "I'm Bert NcNew's grandson," I said. "I knew your brother, Tommy, many years ago. We used to play in the creek down there when we were about your age."

Suddenly his face lifted, "You knew Tommy..." he said. A statement more than a question. "Mister, I sure would appreciate it if you'd not turn me in. I'll give you this here deer. I didn't want no big one like this anyway. I just wanted some venison 'cause pa's down in his back an' can't hunt, an' if I get a deer, I can say he came from our place an I won't hafta buy no license."

"Well that's your buck, Clint," I told him, "and I'll help you gut him and get him to your property. But I think you should ask Mr. Stillwater's permission to hunt here."

"Oh, I did, mister," the boy hung his head again. "but he told me if he caught me in here, he'd skin me alive. He an' Pa don't get along..."

I missed the first two hours of deer season helping Clint drag that buck back to his property line, and I felt something like a cattle rustler. But there were three of Tommy's younger brothers and sisters still at home and the venison would help to feed them.

As we rested and admired the buck, the boy apologized for ruining my hunt, and we talked some more about his older brother. Clint never knew him. He was born the year his brother died.

"I'm moving back up here this year," I told him finally. "Maybe I could get you to work some for me...I'll be needing to hire some help. Maybe eventually I can talk Mr. Stillwater into letting you hunt. But it is wrong to hunt on another man's land without permission, son, and it's also wrong to hunt off your own land without a permit. You aren't a little kid any more. You're at the age where you have to decide between what's right and wrong. You'll find that landowners will give you permission to hunt when you convince them you're a responsible hunter and capable of choosing what's right, even if it's not the way you'd like it to be."

With my little speech ended, Clint spoke without looking up. "You gonna tell on me?"

"No, not this time," I sighed, "provided you'll go talk to Mr. Stillwater and get his permission to hunt next time."

As I headed back toward the creek I turned and he was watching me. The past came back so quickly, as I saw Tommy there with a cane pole and an old collie dog. That was 20 years ago. It hurt down deep. I had gone to college and Tommy had gone to war. He'd have made a fine big brother.

"I'll come by and see you soon, Clint," I said with a wave. As an afterthought I added, "You know, you really remind me of your brother...you're a lot like him."

The boy's shoulders squared and his face brightened with a smile from ear to ear. "Mister," he said, "reckon we can go huntin' some time?"

I looked toward the creek and wondered what the chances would be of getting a shot at a deer later in the day. Then I looked back at that skinny kid in an army jacket and broken shotgun with a buck that he'd never be able to drag to the road.

To Stillwater, he was a problem to be dealt with, a low-life kid from a down-and-out family that wouldn't ever amount to a thing.

I thought about it...We were all ready to condemn him for not playing by our rules, but he had little hope of even being part of the game. There was no one to help, to teach, to set an example. Without that, the young boy would probably just become another slob hunter, another poacher, another problem.

Suddenly I realized that getting that deer back home was the least of his problems. He needed my help — and I owed something to his brother.

Finally, I decided the hunting would wait. What's that they always say — another day, another buck.

Chapter 11
The Shoot-Off

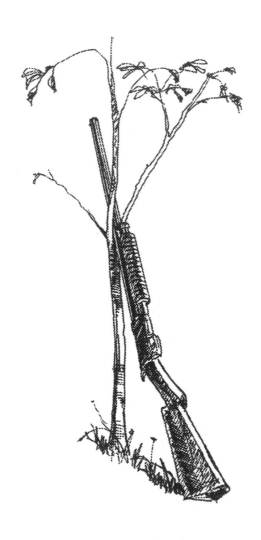

T here were pick-ups all around Sam Venable's old country store. And in the open field behind it, a good-sized crowd was gathering.

There was a chill in the air, and fall colors of red, yellow, gold and brown splashed across the green landscape. You could faintly smell wood smoke in the air, and there were the occasional sounds of shotgun blasts.

A young man stepped from a sedan and savored the sights and sounds of the country. It was good to be home from college for a weekend — back with the people who had raised him, back to a place where time passed slower, and things didn't change much as the years went by.

From the back seat of the auto, he retrieved a cased auto-loading shotgun, and headed toward the field where the occasional roar of a shotgun told him one phase of the turkey shoot had already started. Old timers with long-barreled shotguns were peppering the splatter-boards, each betting his dollar that his gun would put more shot in the middle of the board than any other. The winner would take home a ham or turkey; the losers would try again.

Picking his way through the crowd, the young man passed the familiar faces of neighbors and friends. In this rural community, it seemed there were never any strangers. He responded to the greetings and an occasional slap on the back, passed tables of baked goods and food some of the ladies had assembled, and headed toward the stacks of hay and sawhorses where shotgunners were gathered.

His grandfather sat there on a block of firewood, with two days' growth of whiskers. He grinned when he saw the boy approaching but stayed seated, shifting his tobacco from one cheek to another.

"Hope you ain't here to shoot, Grandpa," the young man greeted him. "I don't intend to compete with no professionals."

His grandfather folded his arms and shook his head, still grinning. He said he couldn't shoot anymore at clay targets. Claimed his eyes were too bad. But everyone remembered how tough he was on flying targets years back. Further beyond him, though, was another old-timer, Jim Anderson, an old friend of the family. Old Jim was his grandfather's trapping partner; he had no grandsons of his own, and when the boy was young, Jim had devoted hours to teaching him how to shoot, fish and trap.

The young man walked up to him and extended his hand. "Heard your old pointer got caught in the neighbors' chicken house again," he said with a grin.

Some of the fellows had turned to listen, and chuckled as Jim's weathered face remained expressionless.

"You young squirt," the old man said with feigned air of indignation, "if yore grandpa weren't my long time friend, I'd commence to thrashin' you for insultin' this country's finest bird dog."

"I hope you ain't here to shoot, boy," the old man went on, "'cause this ain't no place fer no college boy that ain't learned to shave yet, let alone shoot a scattergun."

Smiling, the youngster pulled his new shotgun from its case.

"Jim," he said, "I'm going to let you look at a fine shotgun for once in your life, and don't dribble tobacco juice on it."

The old man took the gun; more attention was centered on the two, and several of the men gazed with envy at the beautifully etched shotgun with the rich, polished walnut stock.

Jim Anderson didn't want to seem too impressed. "She'd look purty in Venable's store winder, boy," he said, "but you get to shootin' it with my ol' 97 an the barrel's li'ble to melt plum away."

Jim's old Winchester was stained and scarred from hundreds of hunting experiences of the kind some hunters only dream of. The hammer was polished, and the forearm worn to bare wood. But it was a long-range gun and Jim Anderson knew how to use it. At these turkey shoots, he had always been tough to beat when the trap-shooting began. Jim always stepped aside after winning a couple of turkeys, because if he didn't, other shooters wouldn't compete.

He was the unchallenged champion at the fall turkey shoots, and it had been that way for years.

"I bought this gun for one reason, Jim," the boy said as he slid the beautiful firearm back in its case. "I've been shooting with it at a trap range back at school and I intend to beat you fair and square today. I've been tryin' since I was 13 and today I'm gonna do it."

"Well now, boy, that there's a fine lookin' gun, all right," Jim said, gaining the attention of a growing number of onlookers. "But I had me a pointer one time that was so purty folks couldn't drive by the house without stoppin' to look at 'er. Trouble was, she didn't point, she didn't retrieve an' she didn't find birds. But she was purty as a pitcher all right, just like that gun of yore'n. Then, I had me a scroungy lookin' ol' dog...."

"I know, I know," the boy shook his head and rolled his eyes. "I remember most every dog you ever had and they were all scroungy lookin.' You're fixin' to tell me your old beat up Winchester can shoot better because it's had more experience, I guess."

Everyone laughed but old Jim. Despite his harsh voice and granite face, folks knew he was enjoying this.

"That purty dog I had barked a lot too, boy," the old man said, "barked and barked an' looked purty an' never did learn to hunt. D'reckly we're gonna find out if you can shoot, er if'n yore best at barkin'."

It came to that, finally, as splatter-board shooting ended and everyone congregated near the trap thrower.

Clay birds were thrown from behind several bales of hay, and there was no telling where it would send the target — right, left, climbing high or whistling along the top of the broom sedge.

Venable required 12 dollars per round, and the winner got his pick of a ham or turkey. Six shooters could put up two dollars each, or 12 men could put up a dollar.

There were better than one hundred people there, nearly the whole community had turned out. The best shooters usually competed first. Others would wait until the really good shots had quit, because Venable wouldn't let anyone keep shooting after he had won twice.

Jim Anderson usually only shot two or three rounds. Word had circulated that Ol' Jim had been challenged, so Sam Venable said it was best to get that contest out of the way. Each man would pay for a box of shells and five dollars apiece.

As with each meet, the shooter took one bird at a time, moving back five yards each round until someone missed.

The boy had been at shoots here before, and local folks knew he could shoot. He had grown six inches taller in no time at all, and he exuded confidence. As a youngster, he had learned to shoot while tagging along with his dad and grandfather and old Jim. When he was 16 he was a good wing-shot, but now he had a trap gun, and no one knew how much time he had spent at the trap range a few miles from his college dorm. This was going to be a real contest!

They both loaded up with identical ammunition and Sam Venable held up two sticks in his hand. The young man picked the long one...old Jim would shoot first.

The old-timer braced himself behind the haystack, gun barrel up and stock down, too proud to hold the gun at a ready position.

"Pull it," he growled, and the trap behind the haystack thumped loudly. A yellow and black clay bird sailed up and straight away like a fat quail. Jim Anderson would never miss a shot like that. His gun stock snapped to his shoulder a second before he squeezed the trigger. The clay bird hadn't gained 20 yards before it ended in a cloud of black dust which fell away in the breeze. Jim's quick shot was risky; it was wiser to let the bird reach 35 yards where the pattern could spread. But he showed his confidence and ability with the shotgun by casually blasting his target out of the air at close range with a tight pinpoint pattern.

The young man would have to follow suit or he'd be behind already, as far as the onlookers were concerned.

He stepped forth and positioned himself, swinging the Browning right and left on imaginary targets. "Coulda broke that last one with a biscuit, Jim. Hope I get one worth wastin' a shell on."

Swinging easily, he wasn't conscious of the rib or

sights on his barrel. He knew he was on the target. He squeezed the trigger, and felt the gun back up against him as the clay bird turned to black powder. The spectators mumbled their approval, and Jim, as he stepped up for a second shot, turned the group to laughter with his terse comment. "Reckon it hit a sumac bush."

Five yards back now, Jim got another bird up, but this one was angling hard to the right and jumping on the breeze. He didn't hurry this one, but blasted it out of the sky at 35 yards.

The younger man looked at one going straight down the middle at eye level. His gun roared and you could hear the lead rattle against the clay just before the bird fell in a dozen pieces.

Again and again they fired and the clay birds turned to falling pieces of black and yellow pottery. The field behind Venables' store echoed with shotgun blasts, and the crowd grew to watch the contest. Finally the two were shooting from 25 yards back. Now the bird was nearly 40 yards away before a shot could be taken.

It had to be quick. Old Jim wasn't talking now. His young friend watched him step to the mark, suddenly realizing that the old-timer wasn't enjoying the match as much as he was. One of the old man's hands trembled ever so slightly, and his concentration was so great it left an impression on his weathered face. To him, it wasn't the turkey at stake, nor the money; it was his pride against the humility of losing at what he was best at. He was thrust to the center of attention, and the thought of losing before his friends was shaking him. The young man could see it.

Suddenly, the prospects of winning didn't excite him as much. Who was he to be challenging this aging hunter who had helped him hold up his first single-shot hammergun.

He thought of years long past, when, as a small boy, he had sat around the stove in Venables' store. listening to hunting stories and asking questions. Old Jim had always been patient enough to answer. And he had taken that same little boy on his first quail hunt...gave him his first puppy... let him hunt on his farm as if it were the boy's own place. In fact, Old Jim's home had always been his second home, the place his dad always found him when he wasn't with his grandpa.

It's not right to challenge him, the young man thought. Not right to take this afternoon from him when he's given me so much.

Jim stepped to the 25-yard marker, looking strained and tired. The trap thumped and the stock of the 97 Winchester snapped to the old man's shoulder in the exact spot it had fallen thousands of times before.

Get it Jim, the boy said to himself. Get it.

The clay bird shot to the left, low and fast. The gun roared instantly and one piece fell from the target, the remainder wobbling into the sumac thicket at the edge of the clearing.

Jim breathed a heavy sigh of relief, then stepped back. His shoulders still sagged. He was not proud of his shot, and he figured now he was beaten.

The young man hoped for a tough one, but he didn't get it. The bird sailed high and straight, fading just a little to the right. He swung on it, then stopped the barrel a split second before his shot. The wadding fell just beyond the haystack, and the clay bird sailed on clear of the shot pattern by a foot, shattering in the limbs of a persimmon tree.

The crowd was too polite to cheer. There were some conciliatory gestures and encouraging words. He shrugged off the loss with a display of disappointment, but deep inside he was elated.

"Jim," he said, "I just got to see if you could have got one more. Try it from 30 back." Thrust into the limelight Jim was the picture of confidence now. He stepped up and broke one last bird from 30 yards back like he'd done it all his life.

"I wouldn't have give a plug nickel for that bird's chances," the young man thought. Turning, he looked squarely into the face of his grandfather. The old man's face was lit up, a big grin spread across it. He didn't say a word, he just winked. He had been watching his grandson, and he knew... the pride in his face showed it.

Jim was enjoying himself now as the men made

ready for more shooting contests.

"Squirt, that there's a purty gun you got" he said with a handshake, "but this ol' 97 here jest growed up shootin' harder 'n' straighter'n anything they can make nowadays."

His young friend made sure everyone was listening to his reply as he said with a grin, "Dang your hide, Jim. That ol' gun of yours ain't fit for much more than a dirt dobber's nest. Mine'll shoot with it any day." He paused a moment, placing a hand on Jim's shoulder. Suddenly his jesting attitude was gone. "I reckon I just forgot about the man behind it."

Ol' Jim didn't say anything, but as he went to get his turkey, his face beamed. The slaps on the back and compliments along the way made his shoulders square up with pride.

The young man dug in for another dollar and a new round of competition. He hadn't known losing could feel so good.

Chapter 12
He Jus' Loves to
Watch 'Em Fly

Billy and I finally gave up and motored back to the boat landing with a lone drake mallard. It had been a cold, clear, flightless morning. I suggested we tie the boat and come back after it. A hot cup of coffee at a small-town cafe not two blocks away would help to thaw us out.

You've been in that cafe if you're a duck hunter, and you've seen the four hunters that were sitting around one table wondering if the ducks were all gone. In every place where you find marshes and lakes and ducks, there are small-town cafes close by, open early for the hunters.

Billy and I shed extra clothing and exchanged pleasantries with the local hunters.

"No darn ducks!" the bearded one said.

"Lost one cripple," said the smaller fellow with the drake curls in his cap and a half-dozen duck-bands on the duck-call lanyard around his neck. He said his favorite spot was froze over solid.. "We were limiting out this time last year right in here."

The waitress brought us coffee and a heavyset man sat down across the counter, wiping his hands on a dish towel.

"Hope you don't want breakfast," he said. "I cooked my last breakfast for today."

Before I could answer, one of the hunters at the table chipped in, "Don't flirt with the waitress, either. That's her pa, an' he'll poison anybody who flirts with his daughter."

The older man grinned at the hunters' laughter. His daughter saw nothing funny in the situation, and she walked through the swinging door into the kitchen.

Boy, I'll bet that girl gets sick of duck hunters, I thought.

The bell on the door rang, and we turned to watch an old man with a half-inch of gray beard walk in, shuffling along in rolled-down hip-boots. He made his way to the washroom, ignoring a comment from the bearded hunter.

I gathered that the old man was a local character by the grins on the faces of the younger hunters.

He reappeared soon, to shuffle over and sit down at the counter next to me.

"Heck, yes, I done good," he remarked to the bearded one. "You fellers forget some of us still know how to hunt ducks."

The cafe owner poured the old man a cup of coffee without being asked.

"How'd you boys do?" the old man asked without looking at either of us. I told him about our only shot.

"Hunt the river tomorrow," he said. "Ever'thing's gonna be freezed over tonight, so they'll go to th' river."

"Link, you still usin' that ol' double-barrel?" one of the hunters behind us asked.

The old man seemed to sense a lack of respect from the four younger men. Speaking to me, he answered them.

"I got an old Stevens double-barrel that'll reach out an' get 'em," he said. "Twenty-six years I had that ol' gun... 26 years, an' I wouldn' t use one a them fancy three-shooters fer nothin'. They won't shoot with my ol' two-holer."

Slurping his coffee, he finally looked us over. "You boys is new here," he said. "We had pretty fair huntin' around here two, three weeks back."

The heavyset man across the counter refilled our cups. "Can't figure you goin' out there on a day like this," he said, "'specially alone. Link, I worry about a man your age out there day after day. Why do you always hunt alone?"

The old hunter's face snapped up; his eyes seemed to sparkle. "Alone?" he said, "...alone? Heck, Rudy, I don't hunt alone. Fifteen years now Ol' Crockett's been in every duck blind I ever hunkered down in."

Rudy moved away to other work, so the old man turned again to talk with me.

"Crockett's my dog," he beamed. "Chessie I think he is, but ain't got no papers or nothin'. Ol' Crockett ain't one a-those dogs that wins ribbons; heck, I wouldn't have all the trophies an' ribbons in th' world. You know, mister, you might have a dog out there that can fetch in three ducks while ol' Crockett gets one. Tell me he can count to 10 on one paw an' I'll not doubt you a bit, but darned if I wouldn't druther have that ol' dog sleepin' at my feet than any duck dog ever was, or ever will be."

The old hunter's face was aglow now, his shoulders high as he sat squarely on the counter stool with the coffee cup lifted in both hands. I nodded in agreement; this old man and I had a lot in common. But it didn' t seem to be a time to tell him about my Labrador. I think he sensed that I knew how he felt.

"I never seen a perfect huntin' dog," he went on. "Heard about plenty of 'em. That boy sittin' at the table there claims his dog works like a goldarned machine. Heck, I know better. Wouldn't matter none to me if he was a reg'lar champeen though, I'd keep ol' Crockett."

He set the coffee cup down and turned his back to the counter, leaning against it as he gazed out the window into a half-a-dozen winters past, picturing, I'm sure, the marshes and rivers of countless hunts and remembering a warm muzzle against his hand as he huddled in a makeshift blind, eyes toward a working flock.

"One time," he said, in a slow and soft voice, "one time I dropped three drake pintails in the decoys with two shots. I was so darn tickled I can't tell ya. Well, ol' Crockett brought back two of 'em and sat there waitin' fer me to tell 'im what a fine job he done. 'Course I was waitin' for him to get that last un, but by darn he wouldn't. Made me so bloomin' mad I finally just waded out an' got 'im myself.

"'Crockett,' I says, 'if I gotta go get one of 'em, I jus' might as well get 'em all!'"

The four hunters at the table were quiet now, and they were listening, as intent upon his words as I.

The aging duck hunter's eyes were moist, but set like bright stones in a grizzled, weathered face. His gaze was fixed, distant.

"I never did tell ol' Crockett what a good job he did on them first two drakes," he said. "An', heck, he only heard two shots. How could a poor dumb animal know you could drop three ducks with two shots?"

He stood finally and fumbled for some change.

"I'd like to get this," I said. "Don't often meet a man

with an appreciation for good retrievers."

"Oh, heck, boy, I ain't sayin' Crockett's a good one, don't y' see? He's jus' mine — good some days, fair some days but *my dog*. They's lots better, I know, but me, I wouldn't have no use for a better dog, long as I got ol' Crockett. An ol' Crockett wouldn't want no better duck hunter to go with, neither. Lord knows they's some better, but it ain't none of these here fellers, for sure."

The men at the table just grinned. The old-timer thanked me for the coffee and shuffled toward the door.

"Say, by the way," I asked, "how did he do today — your retriever?"

"Oh heck, boy, he's old," the old man replied, shaking his head. "I wouldn't send him out in the cold water no more. He just sits there beside me now...watches 'em fly. He jus' loves to watch 'em fly," he repeated as he closed the door behind him.

The waitress was ready to pour me another cup, but I turned it down. "I think I'll got out and ask if I can get a picture of that old man and his dog," I said. "Reckon he'd mind?"

"No, don't do that," her dad replied from behind the counter. "He has no dog now. Ol' Crockett broke down last summer, and the vet had to put him away. We hoped he'd get another. Ain't a man in the county wouldn't give old Link a pup. But he don't want another dog. He's still got old Crockett."

Billy and I returned to the lake to load the boat, and I let Beau, my yellow Lab, out to run a minute. A flock of geese flew by, talking to one another as they passed. Beau watched at the water's edge, his attention fixed on the birds.

"Reckon you'll ever get to retrieve another one, Beau?" Billy said. "It's been pretty bleak lately."

"It'll get better," I answered for the young dog. "And even if it doesn't...we still jus' love to watch 'em fly."

Chapter 13
Painter Creek Buck

Nearly 40 years of Novembers had passed since the first buck was hoisted on the cross pole at the camp on Painter Creek. Everett, Marshall, and Butch were now grown men, taking over the heavy chores that they had watched their fathers perform when they were youngsters and just learning to hunt. Soon they would bring their own children to that hallowed spot, where their grandfathers had gathered before them to hunt white-tails and remember their own happy days of boyhood.

Everett McCausland's grandfather, Anson McCausland, had hunted until his death in his mid-60s. He owned much of the land along Painter Creek, and it bordered national forestland that stretched northward for miles. Marshall and Butch Jamison were brothers, their grandfather had been a close friend of the elder McCausland, and he had hunted the Painter Creek valley until his death only a few years before.

Then, there was old Albert Thompson. Albert, in his 70s, had worked as a farmhand for Anson for nearly 40 years. He had been at the first deer camp, and nobody in camp could remember a season he had missed. Albert had no family; the descendants of McCausland and Jamison were like sons and grandsons to him. The old man hadn't hunted much in recent years. But he came to camp each fall to be with the only friends he had, and to tell stories of deer hunts and deer camps from years gone by.

"It's changed some for shore," old Albert said, sipping a cup of camp coffee and edging closer to the fire as the moon rose on the eve of another deer season.

"When we wuz yore age, all we ever had wuz a couple of ol' army tents and some blankets to crawl under. Why, these here campers an' soft mattresses an' sleepin' bags as warm as toast makes a feller soft."

Everett, Butch, and Marshall glanced at one another and grinned. Les Jamison, Butch and Marshall's dad, smoked his pipe and relaxed in a lawn chair. He could remember those old days. "'Wouldn't you hate to have to sleep in those ol' leaky tents again Albert?" Les asked.

The old man laughed. "I recollec' back just after the war, when you wuz a boy," he began, "when thet big rain hit right in the middle a' the hunt. The crick ain't never been higher than thet, boys...Why, we barely got outta here with our gear."

"I remember!" Les reminisced. "We lost some cooking utensils and some grub. When the rain stopped, I got my first buck that season."

Now that everyone had joined the circle, Albert would get around to telling about how his dad killed a painter on this very creek....the word "painter" was backwoods terminology for panther, and future generations would probably wonder how "Painter Creek" came to be. Albert knew how most of the creeks had come to be named. Finally, it was time for the story — the one Albert told at every deer camp. About the biggest deer he had ever killed, the 21-point, 300-pound white-tail he had bagged in 1922.

The story was relayed detail by detail, and it never varied. Albert insisted a newspaperman took a picture of the deer, and he was always going to try to remember to bring that picture to camp...if he could find it. No one ever pressed him to do it. They always smiled and winked and enjoyed the story, not wanting to tell Albert that the local newspaper had only been in operation since 1926. That night, Albert seemed to be able to remember better than ever before. The buck, with his mammoth rack, was burned into his memory. But boredom became too evident that night. Perhaps Albert noticed for the first time the smiles and head shakes of the younger men. When the story was finished, there was silence for a while. Such a pause wasn't normal; Albert usually went on to other events and happenings. But, that night, he rose to turn in early. As he did so, he spoke:

"You young bucks don't believe me. I know it sounds like a tall tale, an' I prob'ly wouldn't believe it, neither." Again, there was silence. The young men wondered what they could say, wishing they hadn't been so open with their amusement.

"But, they was a big buck," Albert said, "twenty-one

116

points, an' better'n 300 pounds,...I wish to gosh I could think to find that pitcher — then ever'body wouldn't think I'm just a story-tellin' ol' fool."

The men took special pains to make it up to Albert. Over the next three days, he was treated as an honored guest. The climax of the hunt was the fork-horned buck that the old man killed on the last day, his only deer in the past six years.

During the following summer, Albert died in his sleep, perhaps dreaming of deer camps and big bucks. Les, Everett, Marshall, and Butch were pallbearers, and they helped lay the old man to rest in a quiet secluded rural cemetery only a few miles from where he had been born.

"We'll miss ol' Albert," Everett said later when the three young men were together, "but I'm hoping he's some-where with our grandfathers right now remembering the good ol' days."

Marshall smiled, "He's probably telling 'em about that 21-point buck and wondering where the picture went."

"I wonder," Butch pitched in, "if someday, when we're old, if we'll tell stories about bucks we didn't kill and remember experiences that live only in our imagination."

"Maybe that happens when you get older," Everett

surmised. "I don't think ol' Albert meant to tell any lies. I think he really believed all those stories. To him, at least, they really happened!"

At the deer camp on Painter Creek that fall, it just wasn't the same. A generation had passed. Now, Les was the old man in camp, and Everett McCausland brought his 12-year-old son to camp for the first time. When the chores were done, and the campfire burned high, they sat and rested, in anticipation of the events that the dawn of a new day would bring.

It was then that Les brought out the cedar box. "It was Albert's," he said. "He left everything, and there wasn't much, to me. But in this ol' box, I found something that I've waited until tonight to show you boys."

Les brought forth a yellowed newspaper clipping. He took it from hunter to hunter, and with the aid of a light, all could read its message. It told of a traveling newspaper reporter from the city happening across a local hunter with a monstrous buck, a 21-pointer with antlers heavy and wide-spread. As the clipping passed from one to the other, Marshall, Butch, and Everett sat staring into the fire. The clipping left little doubt that Albert's memory had been accurate. He could have been no older than 19 or 20 in the photo, but the paragraph below the picture gave his name and a few of the details that each of the men had heard before, around the fire each November. At the top of the clipping, the date read: December 16, 1922.

Things were quiet at the camp on Painter Creek that night. The three younger men stayed up a little later than usual, after everyone else had turned in, but the there wasn't much said. The memory of old Albert Thompson would go with each of them to their stands at dawn.

A light frost settled over the landscape as the campfire died slowly to orange embers. A coyote howled across the creek as a half moon climbed above the timbered hills.

On the headwaters of Painter Creek, a big buck crossed the trickle of water. Pausing for a moment to test into the air currents, he held his head high, and a majestic set of antlers gleamed in the moonlight.

Chapter 14
The First Gobbler

Hints of light spread across the eastern sky, silhouetting the branches of the big oaks and sweet gums against the coming sunrise.

In the last minutes of predawn darkness, Grandpa stopped and listened. Then he cupped his hands to his mouth, threw his head back, and emitted a loud and perfect imitation of a barred owl. Almost instantly a gobbler answered on the ridge ahead of us, and then another not far from the first.

I was startled; 'til then I hadn't known the reason for the predawn trip across the creek three days before the turkey season opened.

Grandpa hadn't said much, so I just followed, getting a boot wet in the creek with strides too short to reach the rocks that were sticking up out of the current.

I wouldn't ask questions, not wanting to seem like a green kid. I just followed those sturdy, quiet strides and the glow of the carbide lamp and waited.

Now, the stillness broken by the gobblers, Grandpa turned to me. "Near a week now, you been askin' me was they gobblers back in these woods. Reckon now you know."

I shivered a little and wished it was opening day. "They sound a little like beagles on a rabbit trail, don't they?"

"Never heard it put that way," he answered, "but I 'spect they do a little. You'll work that call harder now, knowin' they're out there. You make that thing soun' like a cedar box an' you'll not see nothin' resemblin' a gobbler. Make it soun' like a hen turkey an' you can choose twixt them two."

It was daylight by the time we reached the little four-room cabin across the creek. Grandma had side-meat, oatmeal, white gravy, and biscuits on the table, with home-churned butter and tomato preserves.

As I covered steaming biscuits with gravy, I asked, "Grandpa, how come them gobblers answered the call of a

121

hoot owl?"

Hunched over a piece of side-meat with both elbows on the table, he gave me a look that said he'd rather eat and answer questions later, but with a mouthful he replied, "Reckon they'd of yelled back had I hollered help! Gobblers got a peculiar habit of gobblin' just 'fore dawn when they hear a sudden loud noise. Ketch 'im just 'fore he leaves the roost an he'll holler back at dang near anythin'."

I caught the bus that day and went to school. Grandpa was splitting wood for the cook stove when I left, and he reminded me to practice with my call.

I hated to go to school when there was so much I could have learned from him there on the creek, like setting a trap to drown a mink, or a trotline to catch a catfish, or how to make a call to fool a turkey.

I spent all that weekend at home with my parents, several miles from Grandpa's cabin on Brushy Creek. With chores done, I'd spend all my extra time working that cedar box, trying to perfect the notes of a hen turkey.

Everyone gathered at the Brown Hill country church that Sunday, the day before the spring turkey season. I couldn't concentrate on the preacher's sermon; I kept thinking of those two gobblers that morning in the hollow across the creek.

At the edge of the church lawn, dog's tooth violets were blooming, and the redbuds added splashes of pink to the surrounding woodland. Dogwoods were just opening their white blossoms, and other trees were showing green buds. At night you could hear the flocks of geese passing over, bound for northern pastures. Young squirrels had been out of the nest for awhile, and the spring peepers made the warming nights reverberate with life. It was late enough, Grandpa said, for the turkeys to mate.

At 13 years of age, I had never killed a gobbler. In fact, I hadn't seen more than a half-dozen. In the southern Missouri Ozarks where I grew up, there weren't many turkeys. For years there was no open season on them. Then slowly, game biologists began bringing the flocks back, first transplanted birds, then broods, then flocks — often up to 10 or 20.

The season was short, and to hunt I'd have to miss a few days of school. Mom objected at first, but Dad said there were things a man ought to learn that weren't taught from books. For weeks, I'd been dreaming of this hunt and now it was only one day away.

Sunday afternoon, Mom drove me to the little cabin on Brushy Creek. When I arrived, Grandpa had two willow poles cut, with 15 feet of line and a big treble hook on each.

Brushy Creek had been high, bank full with the spring rains, yet clear enough to let you count the whiskers on a crayfish five feet deep.

A couple dozen yellow suckers had begun to shoal just above a riffle, at the lower end of a big pool. We tied strips of white cloth on the line several inches above the hook, then threw them in the midst of the shoaling fish. When a sucker got over the white cloth, we were to jerk hard and grab him.

The "yaller suckers," as Grandpa called them, were from one to two pounds and when hooked, fought like smallmouth in that current below.

Finally I had two and he had five. We scaled and gutted them on the creek, and he scored the fish lengthwise with long deep gashes less than a half-inch apart so as to cut the hundreds of long tiny bones into sizes small enough to eat unnoticed.

Grandma took over then, preparing to deep fry them and Grandpa got around to listening to my turkey call.

We settled on the screened-in porch overlooking the creek and I rubbed the chalked lid over the edge a time or two, soon imitating the notes of a turkey hen. It produced strong clear notes, but he frowned a bit.

"Not bad, I reckon, fer just a young sprout. If you run across a young careless gobbler, I allow you got a fair chance, but some wise old tom with a beard long enough to trip over might be considerable hard to fool...'less he ain't done too well with the lady turkeys in the past few years."

I hung my head a little, but Grandpa said as close as I was to having it down, he could polish me up a bit and have me sounding so good all the hens in the woods would be jealous.

couldn't hear much of an improvement, he claimed I had it whipped. After supper we went in the small room in front of the old woodstove and sat down in the hand-made rocking chairs. He had built the cabin himself, and most of the furniture in it. There was no electricity and no running water. The water bucket was filled periodically by water drawn from the well.

Grandpa lit a pair of kerosene lanterns and they cast shadows on the walls where guns and steel traps and trotline spools hung. We'd be going to bed early and getting up early, but first there would be the stories that I longed to hear about hunting and fishing years back when Grandpa was a boy.

Enthralled, I listened as he recalled flocks of 60 to 70 turkeys roosting together back in the early part of the century. He had never heard of calling gobblers, so he and his dog worked out a different way to bag them. He'd find a roost, and with his dog he'd go there about midnight and scatter the flock from the roost.

"Nex' mornin' 'bout daybreak I'd hide myself near that roost an' here they'd come one by one back to the roost to gather again. The hens'd come first, scratchin' and perkin' and watchin', one from one way, next un from another way an' dreckly a gobbler would come sneakin' up lookin' this way an' that."

Grandpa ran a hand through his heavy white hair and slapped a fist down on the arm of the chair.

"Even with my ol' muzzle-loader, I pret' near always got me a gobbler thataway. Some folks think those muzzle-loaders was long-range weapons but let me tell you if a gobbler wasn't within 20 paces, you'd be lucky to kill 'im with a muzzle-loader. Sometimes, the smoke was so thick I'd have to jump aroun' to the side to see if I'd got 'im or not.

"I always dreamed of havin' me a breech-loadin' double-barrel. One day this surveyor feller stopped by Dad's place an' said he'd give a pretty penny fer a good turkey hunt. He said he'd tried an' tried an' couldn't get no turkey. Dad, he was a Frenchman an' couldn't talk plain, but he told him 'Go see dat boy dere, he weel show you how to told him 'Go see dat boy dere, he weel show you how to keel de turkee.'

"Well, shore 'nuff, this feller said he'd pay me well if I'd take him an' two of his friends out on a turkey hunt, an' I said I would. Best I remember, they all had breech-loadin' Stevens double-barrels with big pretty hammers. They slept in the barn, an' I went out that night an' scattered a big flock of off'n the roost.

"Nex' mornin' at four o'clock I woke 'em up, an' they was gripin' an' grumblin' 'bout how early it was. The surveyor asked, 'Do we have to get up this early?'

"'No,' I says, 'You can get up late an' fail like you always do!'"

"Well, I got some coffee down 'em and pretty soon had 'em all three in a brushpile waitin' for light an' them turkeys.

"I told 'em to wait 'til they was a bunch of 'em close so all three could get one — an' not to shoot the same gobbler.

"Well, when them turkeys started comin' back, them fellers got to shakin' so much that that brush-pile was a jumpin'. It's a miracle them turkeys came on in but they did, an' finally they emptied every barrel they had. As it turned out, they all got a turkey, though one feller had a hen.

"I cleaned their turkeys for 'em an' when I got back they was fixin' to leave. The surveyor said he'd be back an' he'd left my pay inside with my ma.

"I went on in an' there on my bed was his double-barrel breech-loader, an' a half-box of shells!

"It was then I commenced to keepin' the family well-stocked with turkey in the fall, and since Ma wouldn't let me hunt another 'til all the meat was gone off the first one, I et turkey 'till I hated to look at it, then paid my sisters a nickel to eat the rest of it."

He stopped a moment and laughed at that memory, then pulled out his pocket watch and examined it. "Quarter to eight," he said, "near bed time if we're to get up at four in the mornin'."

I started to unlace my boots rather reluctantly. By

knowing that in 10 hours I'd be on my stand waiting for that gobbler was too much for a 13-year-old to sleep on.

But Grandpa had more to say in a serious tone. "Reckon I've tol' you all I kin tell you 'bout what to do tomorrer. But 'member that a big-mouth hen don't get many more gobblers than a big-mouth woman gets men folk. Work that call three times, four at the most, then wait 20 or 30 minutes 'til you try it again. If a gobbler gets interested, the best thing to do is keep quiet for awhile an' let 'im look fer that hen. If he moves away, then you can hit it a lick or two again, but don't overdo it."

Grandpa leaned back in his rocker and grasped both arms firmly, head back, staring at the ceiling above the old woodstove. "'Spect I ought to tell you 'bout the first gobbler I ever called up, not long after I got that breech-loader. That surveyor feller got me on to workin' that cedar box call, then I took to makin' my own.

"They was so many turkeys it was easy to call up a gobbler then, 'cept I never knowed much how to go 'bout it. I tried a few times an' failed, then one spring mornin' I hit a lick or two on that call an' a hen went to perkin away right smack behind me. 'Course, I laid my cedar box down to see how she done it, an' I'll be danged if here didn't come a gobbler like the devil was after him, lookin' fer that hen. 'Course he never made it cause I was sittin' smack between 'em!

"That's somethin' to remember boy; if a hen is in the neighborhood callin' a gobbler, she'll get 'im quicker'n you will — just put your call down an' let her do the work."

I climbed the ladder into the attic and snuggled beneath the quilts, sinking into the feather mattress, deep in thought about what tomorrow would bring. I slept sporadically, hearing and seeing gobblers with beards as long as coon tails.

The end of the fitful night came with the sound of movement in the room below and the glow of lantern light filtering through the cracks in the attic. I was up and putting on my boots shortly afterward, and climbing down the ladder to breakfast.

I stepped outside for a moment and let the cool air

hit my face. I could hear Brushy Creek softly flowing below the cabin, and I looked across it through the darkness wondering where those gobblers were.

At the breakfast table, my enthusiasm could scarcely be retained. I asked questions faster than Grandpa could answer them.

"Close is about 30 yards at the most, or wait longer if you can; them gobblers is hard to kill...now 'member what I told you 'bout unnecessary movin'," and finally, "Eat yer breakfast an' quit askin' questions, boy, you'll find out how it's gonna be soon enough."

There was a little over an hour of darkness left when Grandpa smeared charcoal over my hands and face, pulling an' old cap down over my forehead.

He didn't seem at all excited, even though this was it — the morning we'd been talking about for weeks. I filled my pocket with shells, and listened to final instructions outside the cabin.

"'Member what I've taught ya," Grandpa said, "an' have patience."

"You'll be hearin' 'im an seein' 'im long 'fore he's close enough to see or hear. Reckon I'll not be 'roun' to help. I'm huntin' on up the crick 'bout a mile."

Minutes later, I was carrying my dad's old 97 Winchester; I wanted to hurry but Grandpa's teaching had been never to move has'tily in the woods, but always to move slowly and quietly.

Finally, I reached my stand and settled in the thicket, with dew from the young buds showering down around me. I put out my carbide light and loaded the gun in the darkness, easing the hammer to the safety position.

Soon, the sky began to lighten and trees and bushes began to assume shapes in the warm, damp morning. An owl passed overhead without a whisper of wing-beat, and I caught a glimpse of him disappearing as silently as he came, taking with him the remainder of the night. Birds were beginning to flit about, talking to each other as they stirred, ignoring me. My hands shook as I brought forth the cedar box and chalk, wrapped well to keep dampness away. I knew I couldn't practice further. Only a few strokes were permissible now and there could be no room for error.

The first note seemed squeaky, and amplified by the morning calm, but the others sounded good. I waited 20 minutes before trying again, then brought forth my best imitation of a bashful, hesitant hen. Almost immediately there came the yelp of a gobbler on the ridge before me, and my heart leaped.

All the anxiety, all the practice of weeks on end, had come to this. That was him. He had answered my call. My hands shook and I breathed deeply to combat it as Grandpa had told me to do. But there was no defeating that excitement. I knew somewhere in the back of my mind even then, that there was something practice and planning couldn't give me that kept old tom and me apart. Self confidence, closely akin to experience and success, was something I couldn't put in that call.

I looked at it in my trembling hands and took a deep breath. I meant to try anyway and learn through failure.

At that moment, from just behind me, came the sweet clear perk of a hen turkey, and the low clucking and put-put call that would make a tom forget his shyness.

I froze, then carefully, slowly turned. The gobbler answered about then, but there was no sound from the hen. I knew she was close, but the brush behind me was too thick to see through. Grandpa had chosen the stand with openings to the front and left of me for a clear shot, but there was no way to catch a glimpse of anything to the rear.

I decided to do nothing, remembering Grandpa's words about the hen years ago that called in a gobbler for him.

When she did call again she was still in behind me, and the gobbler answered much closer. I swallowed in disbelief and breathed deeply again. That hen knew what she was doing, and I could learn something in listening and waiting, placed by a stroke of fortune between her and that gobbler.

I squeezed my gun and didn't move. Again for a long time, all was quiet, and forest life went on around me After an hour-and-a-half of waiting and listening to the occasional exchange between the two turkeys, I thought I caught a glimpse of the gobbler, way out of range, moving through the forest toward me. I strained my eyes, but there was nothing.

The hen began to talk again behind me, and I saw the gobbler plainly now, running like a race-horse through an opening among the rocks and trees one hundred yards away.

Adrenaline poured and I shook violently as I waited for him to reappear where I thought he should. Again there was silence, and the gobbler did not emerge.

I learned then what a virtue patience was, because I had to muster it to sit out that long agonizing wait. I wondered if the hen had moved away, if the gobbler had sensed something and would not come closer. There was a tremendous urge to try my call but I stopped myself. My grandfather's teachings were too strong. I sat like a boulder, eyes fixed on the opening before me. I jumped when the hen spoke again, and caught a glimpse of the gobbler as he stepped completely into view for the first time, 15 yards closer.

The sun, filtering through the trees in one little place, reflected colors from the big bird that were beyond the competence of any artist. I wanted to raise the gun, but he would have been gone if I made a wrong move. So I let him move closer, and away just a little. As he stepped behind a big white oak, I cocked the hammer and lifted the gun in place.

I can't recall squeezing the trigger, and for once the old gun didn't kick. But there was the blast, and the gobbler thrashing about, flogging the bushes in his death throes. I had no regret that I had not called in the gobbler. My elation could not be contained, and I let out a yell that released the weeks and days and the last few hours of anxiety.

It was years before I knew how Grandpa had been a part of my success that day. He never let me know. But he had been there, with his call and his experience, turning back the yellow pages of time to a gobbler many, many years before. He knew my feeling of accomplishment, and though most of it I owed to him, he felt the moment of triumph belonged solely to me. It was a moment I would never forget nor completely be able to relive.

Chapter 15
A Lesson Never Forgotten

My grandfather was good at making things with his hands. He made his cabin, and his furniture, and a host of other wood projects: tool handles, gun stocks and live traps. He also made john-boats and sassafras paddles, some to use and some to sell.

He could see that I had a tremendous interest in bow-hunting. When I was young I made bows from everything I could find around the house, getting into a passel of trouble on one occasion by tying a string to one of my mother's curtain rods.

Grandpa decided it was time I had a real bow, and he make me one out of sassafras. It was a good one, solid and strong, with probably a 25- or 30-pound pull. I bought five target arrows for a dollar at the Western Auto store, and my dad got me a couple of bales of straw to use as a target backstop.

I was around 12 at the time, and I had hunted ducks and squirrels and rabbits with my dad and grandfather. But soon the old single-shot scattergun just wasn't much of a challenge anymore. Of course, I couldn't hit any flying ducks, but anything that sat real still was a goner when I cocked the hammer.

I guess that's why the bow became such a challenge to me. I never dreamed I'd ever hit anything with it, even the stillest target.

About that time, I saw one of those outdoor films where someone was hunting for pheasant. I think it might have been Fred Bear, but at that age you don't pay much attention to names. I did, however, pay a great deal of attention to the fact that the guy dropped a couple of birds and made it look easy.

In a large field not far from our house, large numbers of "bull-bats," as local folks called them, would circle and feed on the wing. Someday I would learn they were nighthawks, a very beneficial bird which feeds in flight, helping to control the hordes of flying insects. But at that time I saw them only as targets, and I spent hours in that field trying to lead one just right.

The bull-bats were safe. As I remember, I never even came close, but at least I recovered all my arrows. They went up, and came down, and the nighthawks fed as if I weren't even there.

My cousin and I would often hunt rabbits, he with his second-hand fiberglass recurve and I with my sassafras bow. We never got one of them, either, but we came close. We lost some arrows because we just couldn't resist hurried shots at cottontails zig-zagging across fields of lespedeza bordered with blackberry thickets.

In time, I got to believing that Fred Bear didn't really hit those pheasants on the wing. It had to be trick photography.

There comes a time in every young hunter's life when it is more important to kill something than it is to hunt. Eventually I reached that point as a bow hunter. Despite the teachings of my dad and grandfather, everything that should never have been a target became one, from the nighthawks to a stray house cat, a barnyard pigeon flock, and a scurrying chipmunk. I just wanted to get something, anything, with my bow, even though my dad and grandpa would have put an end to my bowhunting if they had known.

Finally one February day, a flock of robins were feeding in the field behind our house. With my sassafras bow and a Western Auto practice arrow, I killed my first bird. It wasn't flying, like the pheasants Fred Bear hunted. Maybe that's why I didn't feel the tremendous sense of satisfaction I thought I would experience. The robin was lifeless and limp and the feathers soaked with blood. I didn't look at him long, leaving him there in the field. I walked away feeling as bad as I had ever felt as a hunter. The trouble was, I wasn't a hunter that day, just a shooter, the kind of person my dad told me never to be.

I could hear his words all afternoon. "No Dablemont shoots anything without a purpose. If you don't intend to clean it and eat it, don't even aim at it!"

Dad had talked often about how a hunter should

have a reverence for life; that nothing God had created should be reduced to a mere target. He said that, in time, I'd learn that hunting was something far above killing. When I discovered that, he said, I'd become a hunter.

That little robin became a tremendous burden for a 12-year-old boy to carry. My shoulders sagged with the weight. Two days later I was watching my grandpa build a john-boat, and I couldn't stand it any longer.

"I killed a robin," I blurted out. "Shot it with my bow a couple days back."

Grandpa put down his saw and leaned against the unfinished boat.

"Figgered somethin' like that," he said, "seein' as how you ain't had that bow for two days. I thought maybe your dad had took it away from you."

"He don't know," I said. "I'm afraid he'd skin me alive."

"I doubt he'd do that," Grandpa said. "You know, years ago some folks down in the deep south killed robins and meadowlarks to eat."

My eyes lifted. "You mean it's all right?"

Grandpa took out his handkerchief and wiped his forehead. "I didn't say that a'tall," he shook his head.

"Those folks ate robins once; they didn't shoot 'em just because they was there to be shot at. Then they made it illegal to shoot songbirds at all because they was declinin' so. You broke the law when you kilt that bird."

The load suddenly got about twice as heavy.

"Your daddy killed a cardinal when he was a boy." Grandpa went on.

"Did you give him a good lickin' fer it?" I asked.

Grandpa crossed his arms and looked off into space, thinking back in time. "No, I didn't hafta," he said. "Now if he'd a brought that bird up to show everybody what a great thing he'd done, I 'spect I would have. But he didn't. He just sat there and looked at it awhile an asked hisself why he done it. Then he tried to forget it for awhile and then he finally broke down an' confessed."

For awhile neither of us spoke. "A feller who's confessin' to somethin' knows he's done wrong," Grandpa said, "he don't need to be punished any more cause generally he's punished hisself aplenty. A good man learns from it, an' he don't make the same mistake again."

"I been wonderin' if that robin might of had babies yet," I said with my eyes on the ground.

Grandpa actually laughed. "Not yet I don't reckon, but it might of had 'fore long," he said with a grin staying on his face. "I wondered that same thing when I was a boy, after I shot a big ol' woodpecker."

I looked up, unable to believe what I had heard. "Oh sure, boy, I made the same mistake when I was a kid," Grandpa told me. "But I came to realize on my own that a man worth his salt don't shoot anything less he intends to use it. You're learnin' that, too, an' that's why you can't forget that robin."

He was quiet again for awhile, and then he spoke. "You'll never forget that robin, son. You'll feel a little bit of that robin ever time you drop a mallard, or look down at a buck deer before you clean it. From now on, you'll be a hunter more and more, and a shooter less and less."

Later that afternoon, Grandpa and I went to tell my dad about the robin, and I figured it would be awhile before I'd get to hunt with my bow. Still, my shoulders weren't as heavy as they had been.

It's been almost 30 years now. The sassafras bow is long gone, and my grandfather has passed away. I still spend a great deal of time with a bow, and I shoot plenty... at styrofoam targets. Occasionally I do stand over a buck that I have brought down, and I do feel that instant of remorse. But not guilt. I'm a hunter now, and there's purpose behind every arrow I release in the woods. I have the reverence for life that my dad often spoke of. And grandpa was right... I'll never forget that robin.

Chapter 16
The Relentless Pursuit

She was gaunt because of her inability to kill easily, but the aging bobcat was a large one.

For years now, she had wandered the upper reaches of the White River valley, and with age and experience, she learned to avoid man, to remain deep in the Ozarks wilderness, away from his homes, his dogs, and his cleared ground where nothing lives. And in leaving this, she had learned to survive.

But a winter before, returning to her lair as the night faded, to rest after hours of hunting, stalking and waiting for prey that seemed always harder to find, it had happened. There was no warning, no scent, no sound of man. Then suddenly, there was a noise like thunder and a bullet tore through her flanks. Searing pain shot through all of her hindquarters. She was knocked violently to the ground, snapping at the sudden pain as if it were the attacker.

As she turned and fell, rolling down the slope, there was another explosion, and a bullet smacked into a lichen-crusted boulder beside her, smashing it and sending splinters of rock showering around her. Then she was at the bottom of the slope, where a small stream of water fell along more strewn rocks past a low outcrop of rock. She pulled herself to the ledge and found an opening beneath it. It was not a large opening, but the passageway extended far back, and into that darkness she pulled herself, fleeing the hurt that was so strong.

In doing so, she saved herself, for now came the strange sound of man's voices and heavy bodies outside the protective crevice. The scent now was strong, a scent she would long remember and avoid.

She lay on her side in the dry earth, motionless in the darkness of the cave, pressed as far into its protective confines as her size would allow. Her breathing was rapid and heavy, but a welcome numbness had replaced the pain in her hindquarters, and the blood slowly ceased to flow and became matted over most of her left side.

137

The bullet had passed through muscle along her side at the back of the rib cage, grazing a section of bone in her hip and ricocheted away, exiting through the back of her upper leg.

For two days she did not move, lying in the darkness racked with pain and fever, tongue swollen and eyes glazed.

During the night before the fourth day, the fever subsided, and the slight sound of the trickling water outside aroused a driving thirst. She pulled herself toward the opening, then, once outside, stood for the first time in three days. She put no pressure on her aching left rear leg, hobbling forward on three legs, ignoring the little flashes of pain with every movement in her determination to reach the water.

The air was much colder, and ice had formed around the edges of the flowing water. The old cat drank heavily until she could hold no more. Then, chilled and shivering with weakness, she staggered back to her ledge and crawled back into the darkness where she collapsed from exhaustion.

During the following day, hunger awakened her. She again left the cave to drink, arousing the pain in her hindquarters, then returned to rest beneath the ledge.

Small flakes of snow were beginning to fall when a movement at the entrance of the cave caught the old cat's eye. She froze and a wood rat scurried past, then with a lightening fast sweep of a forepaw she pinned him to the earth. The wood rat struggled only momentarily with her razor-sharp claws cutting into his spine. The she-cat left nothing, her hunger so great the woodrat seemed but a taste.

For days she stayed in her lair, eating little. The snow, which came, melted away and returned again much deeper, helped her to find what little food she could catch.

She ate several mice, which were slowed by the loose, soft snow and found a sick, weakened rabbit which helped sustain her. But finally, regaining some of the use of her injured leg, she left the deep cave that had saved her and headed toward the river, where Ozarks life centered, and food was easier to find.

As the days went by, her leg healed and became

functional, but the stiffness in her hindquarters hampered her in hunting and capturing prey.

There was more failure now than she had ever known; her speed, slowed ever so slightly, made the difference.

Spring came to the Ozarks, and again food became more plentiful. She now fed off nearly anything, a nest of bird eggs, a terrapin, a frog. There was occasionally a weakened rabbit or bird, or in many instances, carrion.

The mating season had long been over, and she was driven by nature to find a place to give birth to her kittens.

It was by chance she found the old cave again that had given her refuge the winter before. It seemed familiar and protecting; the small confines of the dry cave promised an excellent den for her young.

There she gave birth to two kittens, small bundles of fur ever dependent upon her, and she strongly felt nature's instinct to protect and feed them.

At first, feeding them was not a problem, but as they grew older it became increasingly difficult. Pushed by her hunger and theirs, she lost her fear of man, even though she did not lose her respect for him. Several miles from the cave a poultry farm offered what she could no longer obtain in the wilds: easy prey, and food for her young.

For a month she struck the farm, usually in the predawn light. At first, she took only one bird per raid, then two. Finally, in the excitement of her onslaught, she had killed more than she could take, and her visits finally began to hurt the farmer. There was no malice in her raids. She did it because it was easy food, and without it her young could not have survived. There were other poultry farms in the region, and on these she also began to rely. Where losses began to appear, her prey became protected by closed doors and windows on poultry houses which the bobcat could not penetrate. But always, somewhere, there were big white birds roosting in the early light, too stupid to suspect a predator or react to an attack.

As the kittens grew bigger, the she-cat began to make a name for herself. Traps were set at several farms, but the farmers were not trappers, and she always detected and avoided the steel jaws by recognizing the scent of man, steel and oil.

As autumn leaves turned and the cold winds of fall carried them from the trees, the young bobcats left their mother to lead their own lives and she again was alone.

She left the cave now, denning beneath a fallen tree closer to the poultry farms upon which she had become dependent. But the losses her raids inflicted were becoming too great to ignore, and a few of the farmers went for help. Early that winter morning, she had made her kill, climbing a fence she could not jump, selecting an easy meal and leaving as quickly as she had come, dragging a fat hen with her. As usual she stopped shortly to eat her kill, then rested, cleaning the blood from her fur and paws.

The sun was not yet to be seen, but its morning rays had appeared when she heard the bawl of the hound far behind her on the trail.

This was something she had experienced before, and she wasted no time leaving, heading for the river where she would lose the hound. Making no attempt to confuse her trail, the old cat shortly gained the river and without pause plunged into the icy current. She was a powerful swimmer, and her distaste for the water was less than her distaste for a confrontation with the hound.

She did not cross, but rather swam downstream for several minutes, exiting finally on a log which extended into the water. From there she came upon a tree and via an extended limb, jumped to a protruding rock outcrop 20 feet above the river.

This same trick had worked before. The hound would likely cross the river and perhaps find the point at which the cat had left the water. Then he would trail the bobcat to the tree, become confused and give up the chase. With many hounds, the old bobcat's problems would have ended when she leaped to the rock bluff high above the point where she had left the water. But the big hound on her trail was a veteran, nearly as old as she, and with an even greater reputation.

Settlers in the White River Valley knew of Ben Jenkins' hound — that's why he had been called upon when the bobcat's raids became too much to tolerate.

The hound crossed the river and for 20 minutes worked the opposite bank trying to pick up the trail. When he found it, he was fooled for awhile into thinking the cat had treed. But experience told him to look further; some time later he picked up her trail on top of the bluff which led away into the higher country where he was at a definite advantage. In a cross-country chase, the hound, younger and stronger, would soon catch the cat. His job would be to tree her or hold her at bay until Jenkins and his gun arrived. But the exceptional old bobcat would make it a longer chase than expected. In the Ozarks uplands now, she would confuse her foe by climbing and jumping, back-tracking and leaping from ledge to ledge, boulder to boulder.

It took time for the hound to unravel the trail, and if he did successfully stay with her, it would at least give her time to circle back upriver and cross to the cave, which had come to be her refuge if all else failed. Its deep winding passageway, too small for a man, would be safety. The hound wouldn't follow, for in an even fight, he might well be the loser. Even the most inexperienced hound would usually avoid a confrontation with a bobcat on even terms.

Meanwhile, miles away, Ben Jenkins listened to his hound's booming voice dying in the distance, and cursed the river that kept him from following. He had expected the cat to tree long before now, or turn to face the hound against a rock bluff to be held at bay.

But this one had fooled him, and his main concern now was getting his hound back.

The hound had no thought of his master; he was too wrapped up in the chase. Picking his way along the descending ridge, he was perplexed at the slow and confusing trail, but he was not tiring. With easy, unbroken strides he picked his way among scrub oaks and pines along the boulder-strewn hillside.

The scent was growing stronger, the trail simpler, as it drew back toward the river. She drove on tired, stiff legs toward the cave drawing ever closer. Confident of her escape, she was no longer trying to mislead the hound, and when he arrived at the river, the distance between the two was melting away.

The bobcat was now leading up the hollow she knew so well, where a year ago her flank had been seared by the bullet of a hunter, and where during the past year her kittens had grown to maturity.

She could hear the hound growing closer as she found the tiny stream and scrambled around the rocks and ledges for the opening of the cave. But, as happens when the temperature rapidly cools and warms the earth's surface, with excess ground water undermining the oldest and strongest of nature's foundations, a portion of the cave had given way, sealing the passageway with sandstone and shale. She turned to head back the way she came, confused and tired.

Had there been more time, the cat would have most likely retreated and the hound would have been happy to allow her to do so, advancing at a respectable distance. But the cat was cornered and confused, and as the hound burst upon the scene, she didn't wait for his first move.

Snarling and spitting, she instinctively went for the hound's eyes with her razor-claws. The hound in turn had no time to back away. Surprised by the onslaught, one eye was slashed with claws tearing at his head and neck and ripping one ear. Enraged with pain, he bore in, knocking the cat backward. With the momentum of this assault, he went for the throat as she rolled on her back. Dodging the ripping claws, he missed the throat, but his jaws tightened on the chest of the bobcat.

He felt the bones breaking beneath his grip, but he also felt the hot searing pain as the dying cat frantically slashed at his exposed underside with powerful hind legs.

Ignoring the pain, the hound shook the life from his enemy. Finally, she lay still and lifeless before him.

Racked with pain, the weakened victor lay down to rest and regain his strength. But as the brown leaves grew red with his blood, strength and life ebbed away, and he died there, a few yards away from the big bobcat.

Two days later, a hunter found the hound's remains and he was brought to his owner for a hero's burial, long after to be spoken of in highest esteem as a mighty and relentless hunter.

But the old bobcat was forgotten, returning to the earth from which she came, as a part of it, as she had always been. Her bones were picked clean, scattered and bleached by the sun, and no one in the White River valley would miss her.

Her kind, living for centuries as a part of the valley, would continue to dwindle as more forest fell and as the Ozarks wilderness gave way man's progress. Dwindle...but never die!

Chapter 17
Come November

To a boy of 12, the bridge looked indestructible, as certain to last forever as the granite bluffs that protected the river, as important as the clear, cold springs that fed it. An old iron bridge is adornment to a wild river, especially if it has been there forever.

This one spanned the Big Piney, especially imposing in the early fog of a November morning. Our john-boat bounced through the shoal beneath it and we left the old bridge behind again and again as I grew from a wide-eyed boy bundled against the cold, to a teenager clutching a pump shotgun, shivering with the anxiety of another day's hunt.

It was always there, come November — a certain kind of security, a symbol of the unchanging river. And when I was younger, I didn't realize that it hadn't been there since time began.

We crossed that bridge back in early November of 1959. It clanked and clattered, and I looked down through the missing boards at the river below with a special kind of enthusiasm. One of the biggest days of my life was beginning. In an old, worn plastic case beside me was an almost-new, but slightly used, Iver Johnson single-shot 16-gauge. This would be the first time I hunted ducks with the new shotgun. Dad had taught me the first steps of gun handling during October squirrel hunts, and I was ready to hunt ducks on the Piney.

The river was bathed in beauty. Fallen autumn leaves lay thick on the quiet eddies and slipped through the shoals beside us as we passed beneath the iron bridge. My dad's cousin, Charley, was with us that day, sitting beside me on the front seat of the wooden john-boat; we were just behind the blind made of oak and maple boughs woven into a wire frame. It was a cool, crisp day and we were only a half-mile or so down the river when a pair of mallards took flight.

Charley dropped the drake and, somewhat late, I

sent my first volley in the general direction of the hen. She ignored it, and I sat staring in disbelief as the mallard made a retreat up-river, well above the tree-tops.

In hunting squirrels, the little 16-gauge was the last word. Squirrels within range never seemed to get away. Of course, I had only shot three or four squirrels and ducks were different than squirrels.

Charley's drake was only crippled, and the green-head climbed out on the bank. Charley followed, and the mallard returned to the water as I reloaded the Iver Johnson. In a matter of seconds, the drake dived and began swimming past us, a foot beneath the surface. I fired volley number two. Charley may have anticipated what was coming, because he was safely situated behind a huge sycamore. At the roar of the gun, with the muzzle only inches from the surface, water went everywhere.

"I got 'im, Daddy!" I was yelling at the top of my lungs, "I got 'im!"

Looking back, I can see some humor in that situation, but at the time, Dad did not smile. He instructed me to break down the gun and put it in the boat. His stern countenance told me that if nothing else, I did *not* get the mallard.

After Dad and Charley retrieved the mallard from a drift, we floated to a gravel bar downstream, and Dad explained in great detail what might have happened had that muzzle been a few inches lower. When we floated away, I understood that a lead shot will not kill anything underwater.

It was, as I remember, a great day that November in 1959. We soon had several ducks, no thanks to me.

As much as I consider myself a sportsman today, I recall my intense desire to kill something that day. It's all a youngster really recognizes as important during his first few hunts. As Novembers rolled on, I changed that attitude, I'm sure as a result of my dad's guidance and teaching. But that day back in 1959, I wasn't there to hunt; I was there to kill. By mid-afternoon, I had wasted a half-dozen shotgun shells and had only one ancient fox-squirrel to show for it. The squirrels were always thick along the river, but Dad didn't like to shoot squirrels while duck hunting, because too often we'd scare up a flock of ducks just around the bend.

That was a little difficult for a boy of 12 to accept. A squirrel in the boat seemed far better than a half dozen ducks that flew away just as efficiently when I shot at them as when I didn't.

My chance finally came when Dad spotted a pair of wood-duck drakes sitting on a log a hundred and fifty yards downstream. At that time, one wood-duck was a limit and I suspect Dad knew that if I got one, I was almost certain to kill the second one. Maybe he figured I'd miss again.

As we slipped closer and I peered through the blind at those two beautiful wood ducks, I began to shake. I was aware of nothing else. It seemed to take forever for Dad to paddle me into range, and I was sure the case of buck fever I had developed would cause the ducks to flush.

When Charley whispered an okay, I brought the barrel of my shotgun over the top of the blind, cocked the hammer and fired. I don't remember aiming, I doubt if I did. But at 40 yards, the shot pattern was sufficient and the two woodies became trophies. On my first duck hunt I was a game law violator.

I wish I could say that our family always followed game laws to the letter, but that wasn't the case in the beginning. My grandfather had taught my dad to hunt, and he in turn taught me. Grandpa lived with the river. He trapped it, hunted it, and fished it for a living, meager though it was. Grandpa never had electricity or running water or modern conveniences and he scorned game laws and limits because they were modern day contrivances, symbols of progress and change. Grandpa could remember when the old iron bridge was new, and fish and wildlife were so plentiful that protection from the masses seemed needless.

If you picture him as a game hog, you are dead wrong. Grandpa was a conservationist in his own right, and he had reverence for life that caused him to use what he took from the land with as little waste as possible. He and my father didn't skin ducks as many of us do today. They picked them down to the base of the head and the first joint of the wing and used the down to make pillows and quilts. They also cleaned the gizzard, and when you hunted ducks with Dad and Grandpa, you ate ducks. When you hunted or fished, you took what you could use and nothing more. In my younger years, especially when Grandpa went along, I remember having a few ducks over the limit many times, but I also remember that when Grandpa decided we had enough ducks to eat, the shooting stopped.

As I grew older and became interested in the conservation movement, I told my grandfather that I wanted to be a biologist. And though he argued against it violently, he began to obey the bag limits, at least when I was along. Dad was much less interested in the number of ducks taken. He liked to eat them, but Mom and my sisters didn't, so it wasn't a case of putting meat on the table with each outing. With Grandpa, it always was, because it had always been that way. I don't guess I killed a single duck in flight that first season. But I quite often killed one or two on the water. I never gave any thought to sportsmanship. I did a gosh-awful lot of shooting to bag that occasional duck or two, and when I cocked the hammer on that old single-shot, a sitting duck had a good chance to escape untouched.

On every trip I learned — sometimes little-by-little, sometimes a whole lot at once. I hadn't had the gun long when we witnessed something that few men will ever see.

We had just put in one morning at first light and were only a short distance below the old iron bridge when a ruckus on the bank attracted our attention. I watched a red fox chase something along the bank and then follow it into the fog-shrouded river with no hesitation. The smaller animal swam upstream toward us, with the fox in close pursuit. Suddenly I saw that the fox was after a chipmunk. I cocked the hammer and raised my shotgun with the intentions of saving the chipmunk. But Dad intervened, and reluctantly I lowered my gun. The chipmunk passed our boat only a few feet away, exited near a pile of rocks and was gone. The fox also ignored us, swam past and climbed out on the bank to furiously claw at the pile of loose rock. When we passed around the bend and out of sight, he was still circling the rocks.

I was dejected. I could have bagged a fox with no trouble. Demanding an explanation, I waited while Dad lit his pipe. I never forgot what he told me.

"The fox isn't what we're after," he said as he paddled slowly down the Piney. "I don't hold with shootin' somethin' just to be shootin'."

I half-heartedly argued that I wanted to save the chipmunk. Dad laughed and shook his head.

"Why feel sorry for the chipmunk? The fox is the one that's hungry. Everything has to eat, the Good Lord made it that way. If you consider the fox evil for eating a chipmunk, then you and I are evil for eating ducks.

"In nature," he went on, "there are no good guys and bad guys. That shotgun doesn't make you a judge. Don't cock the hammer unless you figure on eatin' what you shoot."

Slowly, steadily, I grew and learned...and changed.

A month later Dad and Charley and I crossed the old iron bridge again, following the gravel road only a short distance to the put-in point above the bridge. It was a blue, cold day, cloudy and overcast, temperatures in the mid-20s. Dad hadn't intended to let me go that day, but the season was closing, and I hadn't missed a weekend. I was so heavily bundled against the cold I could hardly shoulder the little Iver Johnson, but the ducks were numerous, and I had a drake mallard by mid-morning. Then Charley snapped a boat paddle on a rough, twisting shoal and the john-boat hit a log sideways.

We all went out as the boat tipped and water poured in. I clutched that shotgun and went under. When I came up, Dad had an arm around my waist, and in water over my head, he found solid footing.

On an adjacent gravel bar, my clothing turned stiff with ice, and I was sure I would die. Dad and Charley wasted little time pulling wood, twigs, and leaves from a nearby drift and, with a cigarette lighter brought along for just such a situation, Charley started a fire that was a roaring blaze in only a few minutes.

Our boat had not turned over. Filled with water, it had been pulled to the gravel bar. The only thing that was missing was Charley's shotgun, a new automatic Winchester.

Dad told me to strip off to my insulated underwear and dry my clothing. I couldn't believe he actually thought I could live through such an ordeal, but I did what he said, and stood there roasting wet clothing over the open fire, freezing on one side and toasting on the other. I watched Charley wade out into the swift, shoulder-deep water, and dive three times before coming up with his gun. I was sure he must be the toughest person in the world.

In November of 1976, Larry Dablemont and his Labador, Beau, float below the new bridge on the Big Piney River in one of the family's old wooden john-boats.

In less than two hours we were dried out and back on our way. In years of hunting the river we never dumped a john-boat before or since. That's a testimony, I believe, to the stability and strength of those wooden boats.

The years went by and Dad and I continued to hunt the Piney, come November. I slowly began to realize that these hunting trips were worth much more than the wild duck meals they provided. It was especially good when my grandfather would hunt with us. He'd take his old double-barrel; but in his 60s, he began to lose interest in shooting ducks. I marveled at the way he cleaned game so quick and effective. Dad could pick, singe, and clean a duck in short order, but Grandpa was able to prepare a duck for the oven quicker than anyone I've ever met.

He was even more strict about gun safety than Dad. That seems strange when you realize that he raised four sons on the river, and each of them was hunting on his own when he was 11 or 12 years old. In his home, Grandpa kept every gun loaded, always. They were kept on a high rack with barrels pointed into a corner. My dad and uncles never picked up an unloaded gun, and while it certainly isn't an idea most sportsmen would accept, things were different in the south. Grandpa was never surprised to find a gun loaded; he expected it, and he insisted I handle my single shot always as if it were loaded.

As I grew older, progressing through high school, the old iron bridge became so rickety they placed a sign upon it: "Bridge unsafe. Cross at your own risk." Boards were missing everywhere, and crossing was truly an adventure. Dad said he had heard talk about a new bridge and a paved highway. But I paid little attention. I was more interested in hunting with my new pump shotgun, a model 12 Winchester. Dad paid $50 for that gun. He owned the local pool hall in the small town of Houston; it was a hangout for local farmers and rivermen, and I worked there after school. I took that Winchester in to show it off just after I got it, and it prompted lots of stories about fine old guns and experiences. Those stories from a host of front bench regulars were the highlight of my day. Those old men became closer friends than schoolmates with whom I had little in common. I treasured their advice and opinions.

My teachers occasionally voiced their opinions, too.

Some didn't think a youngster should be allowed to sit on the front bench and read *Outdoor Life* magazines while homework was shoved behind the Coke machine. Some thought I missed a lot in those days. My grades were mediocre. I never attended football games or parties. And my days in school dragged by, come November, as I watched the clock and counted down the hours until Friday night. The best part of life began on Saturday morning, November the first — crossing that old iron bridge.

The wild ducks that stopped to rest and feed along the river fascinated me from boyhood. There were so many species, so beautiful in every respect. And they were all travelers from the northern wilderness, land of timber wolves and moose and bear and all those things I was sure I would never see.

To a youngster who had never been out of southern Missouri, those lands seemed so very far away; I never dreamed I 'd be able to go there. Now that I 've hunted and fished in many states and Canada, I realize there never was any place like the Big Piney. Maybe the ducks thought so, too — especially the wood ducks.

In 1963 I killed my first banded duck. Dad and I were floating through a big eddy two or three miles below Slabtown, when, in a little pocket at the lower end, I caught movement among the fallen leaves.

We carefully stalked them, and at 35 yards the flock of 30 woodies took to flight. I dropped one drake, and when I picked him up, I couldn't have been more elated if that band had been solid gold.

For weeks I rushed to the mail box daily, awaiting the banding information from the Fish and Wildlife Service. Finally it came, telling me that my wood duck had been banded the previous spring in Onalaska, Wisconsin.

I had read many articles about Wisconsin and Michigan in *Outdoor Life*. A fellow named Ben East lived up there, and I always read his articles first. I dreamed of being an outdoor writer just like him some day, and I wondered if maybe Ben East might have hunted a northern marsh a few weeks before when that same flock of wood ducks had passed by. Probably not, but at least those ducks had been there, way up in the distant northern wilderness of Wisconsin.

We often saw deer on the Piney, crossing just a few yards in front of our blind. But in 1964, on a float just above Slabtown, on a shoal a few hundred feet below Paddy Creek, a giant of a deer walked majestically to the water's edge and crossed with his head held high. That rack was unbelievable, and though I had never seen a live mule deer, I recognized that one as such from stories and photos in those old magazines. He finally scented us when we were only 20 or so yards away and drawing closer with the current. With the magnificent head held high, he gracefully bounced up the steep hillside and disappeared into the timber. Of course, there are nothing but white-tails in the Ozarks, and no one ever believed I had seen a muley. That's when I began thinking of hunting with a camera.

It's hard to describe the thrill I felt when Dad once paddled up on a big mature eagle bathing himself on a shallow shoal. We floated to within a few yards, and he flew up onto a snag where he fluffed the water from his feathers and stared down at us as we passed, indignant at having been disturbed.

Those steep Ozarks river bluffs were inhabited from the late '50s until the late '60s by wild goats. They were shaggy, white animals with big curving horns, descendants of tame goats released into the wild, so Dad thought. Once, we heard what sounded like rifle shots a mile or so downstream. Eventually, we rounded a bend to a most unusual sight. There, on a hillside so steep a man would have had difficulty standing, two big rams were hurling themselves together, butting heads with a resounding report that carried up and down the river valley. They stepped back a few yards and launched themselves forward with driving back legs.

We passed, and they paid us little regard. Four or five ewes that were watching seemed bored by the contest, but apparently it continued, because we heard those horns meet for another 30 minutes as we moved down river.

The goats are no longer there. We wonder if some poorly taught deer hunters may have used them for target practice.

In the late '60s, we noticed that the National Forest surrounding the lower Piney attracted increasing numbers of deer hunters from St. Louis and Kansas City. On opening weekend of deer season in 1966, as we floated through a big eddy, three rifle shots rang out and we could hear dying slugs whining over our heads. We let the shooters below us know we were there, and we passed a riverside deer camp where three "hunters?" were firing high-powered rifles at a whiskey bottle in the river while working on draining another bottle.

As we passed, I remembered that at only 12 years of age, I had learned what happens when a projectile is fired at the water's surface. Year after year, the numbers of shooters increase during deer season. For thousands, it is the only hunting they do in the course of the year. No wonder landowners are upset with some hunters. No wonder anti-hunters are gathering fuel. Our ranks are deteriorating as they grow.

In the second half of the 1960s, I attended college, spending most of that time at the University of Missouri studying to become a biologist — except on weekends, when I returned to float the Piney. Finally the new bridge was finished and the gravel road closed.

At that time, as we floated beneath the old iron bridge, I was in the back of the boat with the paddle, repaying Dad for all those years when I went along for the ride.

I began to realize that change is a part of all things. The river changed its course, with shoals and eddies moving drastically from year to year. But the quick change brought about by man was usually bad for the river and the fish and wildlife that lived in and along it.

Landowners began to cut the giant white sycamore along the banks to sell the logs to be used in making crates. Gravel operations along the river made big money for some people, but erosion from unprotected banks and filtation from gravel operations filled the large eddies quickly. Some of the holes that were 15 feet deep in the early '60s were only five feet deep by the late '60s. Huge boulders on the bottom that had harbored smallmouth were covered by sand and gravel. As that happened, folks wondered why the fishing

Grandpa, who wanted only the river and his free-dom, sensed the attitude of the Ozarks landowner changing as real estate people began to advertise the Big Piney country in cities around the midwest.

Looking at a row of stumps where huge sycamores once shaded the river, he told me something I'll never forget:

"They all say love is what makes the world go roun'," Grandpa said as he paddled, "but money will stop everything in its tracks someday. Nothin' stronger in this whole world than human greed."

Not long afterward, a landowner on the lower Piney bulldozed a small buffer strip of trees into the river just to gain a few more feet of pasture land in a river bottom a half-mile wide. More than four miles of river bank were leveled in a couple of days. With the trees gone, there was nothing to hold the soil, and the erosion of that cattleman's land continues today. He cusses the river for it and declares that a dam should be built to stop the flooding.

On November 1, 1970, my first daughter was born. That's the only opening November weekend on the Piney that I have missed. A couple of weeks later Dad and I floated the river again, but it was something of a solemn occasion. Grandpa was in a St. Louis veterans' hospital with cancer. Only a few months before, he had been on the river as always. The fall before, he had hunted with us.

That day, as I floated beneath the old iron bridge, I realized that someday the Piney would flow on without it. I hadn't really thought about that before. When my little girl was a month-and-a-half old, and the 1970 duck season ended, Grandpa passed away in the St. Louis hospital. The following year, the old bridge was demolished to prevent someone from being hurt on or beneath it.

Dad and I continued to hunt the Piney. On happy occasions in the fall, Mom and my wife and little girl would come to pick us up at the new Slabtown bridge when we made the upper float.

Once, I walked out on the big steel-and-concrete span with my daughter, then four years old. I held her up and she tossed a rock into the river far below, giggling delightedly.

This fall, I'll take my daughters, now 15, 14 and seven on another float down the Piney. The big bridge fascinates them, and I think back on the old iron bridge that so enthralled me when I was young. I'll show them those concrete and iron abutments a half-mile downstream where the old bridge once stood. It's covered with vines now, and young sycamores are trying to hide it from view.

My daughters might wonder why I'd even point it out. But it will be a good opportunity to tell them that things change. Maybe I will show them that the river, and life along it, are more valuable than we might realize and convince my daughters that we shouldn't use a dollar bill to measure anything.

Their grandpa could help. He could point out the place where ol' Dad learned that you can't shoot a shotgun under water.

And maybe, years from now, I'll be fortunate enough to take my grandson down the Piney, come November, and there'll be new sycamores to admire, and a few squirrels and ducks to hunt. Maybe he'll look in awe at that steel and concrete bridge that spans the Piney today and never question that it will be there forever.

Chapter 18
Miracle on a Snowy River

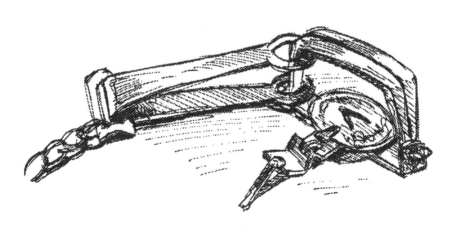

I t wasn't much more than a shack at the confluence of two small Ozarks streams, but it would serve as a one-night shelter for the trapper, on his way home after a week on the river. It was late evening, and the snow had been falling since midday. The old cabin was a welcome retreat for the man who had slept in river-bluff caves for the past several nights. With Christmas only a week away, he was headed home with a disappointing catch.

He hadn't expected to have company, but as the day dwindled and the snow grew heavier, another john-boat drifted downstream out of the gathering darkness, at it's stern an aging riverman who looked to be another trapper. The two met at the gravel bar as the younger man filled a bucket with water for the night.

"The name is Ansel Wilson from Jerome Crossing downriver," the older man said as he stepped from his boat in hip-waders, "I got behind a bit, expected to be down to the Sand Shoals crossing today. Meant to catch a ride there tomorrow and be home by tomorrow night."

He said he had been trapping up the river for several days, and at the bow of his john-boat a bundle of furs showed he had done well. The younger trapper whistled beneath his breath at the half-dozen mink pelts he saw there — prime, top quality mink that would bring a hefty price at the fur companies in St. Louis.

"I ain't caught but two mink all season," said the younger man. "You must be one gosh-awful trapper, old timer."

The older man smiled and said he had been lucky... at least until he had gotten behind and the weather had set in.

"You're welcome to unload your gear here and spend the night," the younger man said extending his hand. "Jim Mallory is my name, and I don't mind company for the night. Besides, I don't own this ol' shack, an' the feller that did died some time ago. My place is on up the east fork about four or five miles...can't get there tonight in this storm so I figgered I'd set it out here."

As darkness came and the snow swirled outside, the two men heated canned beans and coffee on the small wood-stove, and blocked the cracks where the cold wind came through.

"Woulda hated to spend the night on the river tonight," the old man said. "I'm nigh onto 65 years old. Can't take what I once could... How old are you, boy?"

The younger man's grim face lightened just a bit, "I ain't exactly a boy," he said. "I was born in 1901, I'll be 35 next spring...feel like I'm older than you."

"You appear to have the weight of the world on your shoulders, son," the old man said. "Are you all alone at your age?"

"No sir, I ain't," came the reply. "I got me a wife and two youngsters waitin', and another boy who ran off last spring, only 16 years old. Ain't seen nor heard from him since...figger he's gone for good. Maybe better off than if he'd stayed home. Times gettin' harder, I'm fixin' to lose my place on top of all that."

"Sounds like you are carrying a powerful load, at that, son," the old man said in a sympathetic, comforting voice. "But things aren't usually as bad as we make them to be in our mind...and you're young and healthy, with good days ahead."

The young trapper rose, somewhat disgusted with that line of reasoning, and added some wood to the stove. "You sound like my wife. She spends most her time in church, prayin' for better times, for our boy to come home. I work, she prays, and nothin' good ever comes. Maybe God has too many people to listen to, but he don't seem to hear her. Ain't seen no miracle yet."

The older trapper was quiet for awhile. When he spoke, his voice seemed changed somehow.

"Maybe you expect too much too soon," he said. "It took most of 60 years for God to work his miracle in my life. But it came one night on a river bank not far from here, and overnight I became a rich man only because I became a new man. You appear to give up easily, while you're wife

160

Angrily, the young man turned, and spoke with a flame in his eyes and a voice hot with resentment.

"Give up easily! Mister, I've worked this river for weeks, doin' the only thing I know, and I've caught two mink. Muskrats and coons don't bring the money I need, and prayers don't make fur worth more than it is. They ain't no miracles for little people who work and pray. Miracles are for the city folks who have all they need and can't get enough — the people who hold mortgages, and who own land and fine things. God takes care of them, not people like us!"

"You're wrong, young man," the older man's voice was strong and clear, "and you are full of anger because you think God doesn't know you exist. But He performed the greatest miracle for men like me and you almost 2,000 years ago when that baby he sent to earth was born in a simple manger that would have made this old shack look like a mansion. And whatever comes your way, if you ask for His will to be done, it will be sufficient for your happiness and your family's well being. You have evidence of His care for you in the wife He sent your way, and her constant prayers."

It was quiet for awhile, as the younger man weighed the old-timer's words, and calmed a bit. He turned with something of a smile, and dug out an old pipe.

"Well, maybe you are right at that, sir. But I can't help but wonder what kind of miracle keeps you running this old river in the dead of winter trying to trap where the fur is scarce as hen's teeth. I expect maybe I'd be better at recognizing a miracle than you would. I ain't never seen a miracle, but I expect I'll sure know one if I see it."

They laughed together at that, and after a spell of quiet, the young, man puffing on the pipe, spoke again in a more solemn tone.

"But I thank you," he said, "for reminding me of the Christmas story. I hadn't thought of its meaning for some time. It's a comfort thinking that He's watching over my boy somewhere, and that He'll guide him right. That's all I really can ask. I'll take care of the rest, I reckon, with or without His help."

161

His help."

It was too dark to see the look on the old man's face as he shook his head and closed his eyes, and understood.

Eventually, the snow stopped and the wind calmed, and the young man slept as he hadn't slept for a week, on the old mattress on the floor, rolled up in musty-smelling quilts. It was well after sun-up when he awakened, and the fire had burned down in the stove. To his surprise, the old man was gone.

"That old timer musta been in one heck of a hurry to get home," he said to himself, noting there were no tracks left in the four- or five-inch snow. It would have taken a couple of hours for the wind to drift over the sign a man would make, so he had surely left at the first hint of light. He wished he could have talked to the old trapper before he left. He hadn't got to know much about him.

But he brushed the snow from the john-boat and loaded his furs and gear, readying for his last few miles upstream to his family and home. Then he saw the half dozen splendidly prepared mink furs the old man had taken. He had left them for a man he didn't even know, a man who he felt needed them more than he did.

The young riverman sunk to his knees there on the river bank, and shook his head in disbelief. He had never asked for help from his friends, let alone a stranger who had very little for himself. And, despite the good intentions, he could not take charity from anyone. The small town of Jerome was a ways to the north, but he would return the furs and thank the old man for his kindness — and tell him he could make do with his own resources, without a hand-out from any man.

Nevertheless, he thought about those pelts all day as he drew closer to home. There was enough value in those furs to pay his overdue bills and have a little left for Christmas gifts for his wife and kids — something they hadn't had in many years. But that old man had worked hard for those pelts, and he looked as if he needed the money as much as anyone.

Late in the morning, he secured his old john-boat at the small landing. He looked toward the cabin which sat ney and there was warmth, a soft bed and good cooking — a far change from what he had experienced the past week on the river. With his gear and furs unloaded, it would take several trips to get everything, so he packed what he could carry on his back, and with his gun in one hand and the mink pelts in the other, he headed up the long path.

It was then that he saw his wife flying down the path toward him, and he knew in the blink of an eyelash that something was wrong. He dropped the pelts and his rifle, and threw his arms around her as she sobbed, holding him as tightly as she ever had before.

"My God, woman, what's wrong?" he said, pushing her away to look into her tear-streaked face. And then he saw the love that was there. These were tears of joy, not sorrow.

She pulled him tightly against her again, and with her face pressed against his chest she sobbed uncontrollably, "He's home," she said. "Our boy's come home!"

*　　*　　*　　*　　*　　*

Two days before Christmas, Jim Mallory caught a ride to Jerome Crossing without the slightest idea how he would get back home. He wasn't concerned. His steps were lighter now, and he believed finally that whatever was to come, he could handle. His son was home, a different young man than he had been the year before, safe and sound and wiser from the harsh life he had experienced in the city. But as the boy had learned much while he was gone, so had his father. He had learned, for one thing, to believe in his wife's prayers.

Jerome Crossing wasn't a big place. The railroad crossed the river there, and there were several businesses and a hotel. There was a courthouse, and that's where the sheriff's office was found.

"I've come looking for a man by the name of Ansel Wilson," the riverman said as he introduced himself and extended his hand. "I have some furs that belong to him, and I need to thank him."

The sheriff sat down in his chair with something of a skeptical look, and shook his head as he replied, "Nobody ever came in here wanting to thank ol' Ansel for anything ever came in here wanting to thank ol' Ansel for anything before, I don't reckon. I had a few wantin' to shoot 'im or hang 'im, but nobody ever wantin' to thank that old outlaw."

Perhaps he could see the puzzlement on the face of the visitor, so he went on, "But he ain't gonna be easy to talk to anyway, Mister, he's dead.

"Giggers found him froze to death on a gravel bar upriver last winter where he was huntin'. The doc said he figgered he died in his sleep of a stroke or heart attack or somethin'."

At first, Mallory thought he must surely be talking about a different person, but the sheriff brought out an old and tattered picture.

"I arrested this ol' rascal a half dozen times over the past 10 years, for public drunkenness, fightin', stealin' furs. Lordy, he was capable of anything once.

"Then back in the winter of '33 he became a different man. Came in from the river and told everyone that he had met an angel of God on that same gravel bar where they finally found him dead. Everybody thought he was nuts — tryin' to give away fish and help everyone — this bein' the same guy that once stole fish off every trotline he came across and would wheedle a man out of his last cent. All of a sudden he's preachin' on the streets and sittin' in the front pew at church, singin' at the top of his voice and embarrassin' all the ladies."

Mallory started out, "Sheriff, I know you won't believe this, but I met this same man on the river not a week ago, and he left these furs with me." Mallory was looking hard at the picture and feeling like he had been kicked in the chest by a mule. "He was just as alive as me or you, and just as sane."

"Well, then you'll have a hard time believin' this, son, but I went with the doctor to examine the body, and I was there when he was buried," the sheriff said.

"I remember thinking how odd it was to see him froze to death with a peaceful smile on his face, a man who had spent most of his life frownin' and gripin' and fightin'. I knew ol' Ansel, and I think he was a changed man that last

164

year or so, but after a whole lifetime of bein' ornery and worthless, nobody would believe it. He died without any relatives I know of — without a friend."

"I don't know about that, Sheriff," the young trapper said, "the man I talked to had a Friend. And he was at peace."

"Well if you talked to old Ansel, you talked to a ghost," the sheriff told him. "But I've seen stranger things happen in this job, I ain't gonna call you a liar"

As the visitor got up to leave, the sheriff added, "Son, if you've a mind to sell them furs, ol' Jim Baines is set up down at the feed store next to the railroad tracks today, buyin' from some of the local trappers. He'll pay you a fair price, an' I reckon nobody can argue those are your pelts now."

Mallory thanked the lawman for his time and help, but turned before he left, with his hat in his hand and a troubled look on his face. "It must've been a miracle — a man changin' like that before your very eyes."

"Well some might say that," the sheriff said. "Others would say he just got old and went off his rocker. I don't know that I ever seen a honest-to-goodness miracle. And I reckon I'd know one if I seen one...wouldn't you?"

"Yessir, I expect I would," the young man answered, feeling the tingling sensation on the back of his neck as he remembered saying the same thing a week before in the shanty on the riverbank. "I expect I would know one if I seen it!"

He opened the door and started to leave, but something made him turn back.

"I'm 35 years old and I don't remember ever sayin' this to nobody, Sheriff," he said with a grin spreading across his face, "but... Merry Christmas!"

An hour later the young trapper stood on the wood steps of the feed mill with more money in his hand than he ever remembered having at one time; he looked toward the river below, flowing past the small but growing settlement. It seemed like it was indeed a miracle — the money he needed coming so easily, after so many months of struggle. But he knew that there were greater miracles than the ability greatest miracles on earth are the changes in a man's life that make him become what he himself never dreamed he would be. Old Ansel Wilson had experienced such a miracle and he had tried to pass it on to others. In the small town where everyone knew his past, he had experienced little success in the short year he had left.

But in a small shanty on the headwaters of an Ozarks river, on a gray, snowy December evening, he had spread the miracle. He had opened another man's eyes, and changed a life...forever.

*   *   *   *   *

It was beautiful winter day in December of 1962 and the congregation was passing out of a small Ozarks church on Christmas Eve. One of the members stopped to shake hands with the old minister and his wife, and give his comment.

"A wonderful sermon, brother," he said, "The Miracle of Christmas. We too often take the Christmas story for granted, but miracles didn't stop there, did they? Problem is, we just don't often recognize a miracle when it happens... nice to be reminded."

And then, as an afterthought, the church member turned back to look into the beaming face of the old minister. "By golly, I reckon you've seen a miracle or two in your time haven't you, Preacher Mallory."

With a smile, the minister chose his words carefully, gazing off across the countryside as if his mind were somewhere else. "Yessir, Mr. Davis, I expect one of God's greatest blessings is a genuine ability to recognize a miracle no matter how great or small..."

The preacher's eyes moistened just a bit as he thought of the old trapper so many years ago; and as the Davises turned away, no one heard him add beneath his breath "...and I expect I'd know one if I seen it."

For additional copies of
"Ain't No Such Animal,"
Please write to:
Lightnin' Ridge Books
P.O. Box 22
Bolivar, MO 65613